PRAISE FOR MIND OVER MOMENT

"In a world that requires more resilience every day, that path clearly goes through the crossroad of gratitude. Anne shows you how to travel that path and provides insightful and practical [ ] do it. I have tremendous gratitude for Anne and Mind over M

—*Shawn O'Grady, President, Foodservice at* [ ] *eneral Mills*

"Actionable tips and tools for build [ ] capability is much needed, all laid out in a practical [ ] anecdotes and humor."

—*Sam King, CEO Veracode*

"Anne Grady gives us a quick-reading field guide to become resilient in chaotic times. Filled with delightful stories and supported by the latest research, *Mind Over Moment* is the perfect superfood for any soul hungry for peace."

—*Keith Winkeler, VP of Engineering, Dell Technologies*

Mind Over Moment is an ideal book for this moment. Anne Grady offers a clear, compelling framework for how to strengthen your resilience and well-being through bite-sized strategies rooted in mindfulness. A great storyteller, Grady also shows that she has lived these strategies and is passionate about sharing them with us. I can't think of any woman or man who would not benefit from reading this book.

—*Laurie Dalton White, Founding Director, Conferences for Women*

"Bravo for *Mind Over Moment*. I started reading this gem and couldn't stop turning the pages. Anne has given us a crisp, in-depth, actionable way to grow our minds and protect our mental wellbeing. I love this book and can't wait to tell everyone that I know that it's more than a must read; it's a must do."

—*Simon T. Bailey, Bestselling Author of* Shift Your Brilliance: Harness the Power of You, Inc.

"Clever, funny, and practical. Anne Grady's *Mind Over Moment* is an indispensable guide to building resilience."

—*Libby Saylor Wright, Chief Operating Officer, Women's Foodservice Forum*

"Actionable, practical and so timely for the challenging world we find ourselves in today."

—*Nataly Kogan, author of* Happier Now *and founder of Happier, Inc.*

"*Mind Over Moment* reminds us of the beauty that exists within life's struggles. Scientific- and evidence-based, *Mind Over Moment* takes your hand and walks you down a path of mindful behavior, sharing new approaches for experiencing mindfulness in everyday living. This book is not just about harnessing the power within, it's about rebounding from life's punches—and that makes *Mind Over Moment* pure magic."

—*Anne Bruce, Bestselling Author of Discover True North and*
Discover True North Relationships

"*Mind Over Moment* is a major stand-out. In this book, Anne Grady shares practical insights and applications, along with unvarnished examples of her own challenges—ones she has overcome through years of study, intention and strategic action. She brilliantly describes the full spectrum of factors that impact our ability to thrive when faced with adversity and uncertainty. She also provides a clear model, rich with valuable strategies, that shows readers exactly how to move from mindset to skillset to reset."

—*Sara Canaday, President, Sara Canaday & Associates*

"You cannot always control what life throws at you. You can, however, control how it impacts you. Anne Grady provides actionable steps in her humorous style to help you enjoy the delicious moments in life."

—*Elizabeth Lombardo, Ph.D., Bestselling author of* Better Than Perfect:
7 Strategies to Crush Your Inner Critic and Create a Life You Love

"Anne Grady masterfully weaves together a mix of authentic (and hilarious) storytelling and neuroscientific data that compels readers to embrace the life-changing possibilities of mindfulness and then provides practical and easy ways to harness its power. From "delicious moments" to "lighthouses," this book takes you on the pathway to building the resilience we all need to survive life's challenging moments!"

—*Karen Ranus, Executive Director, National Alliance on Mental Illness (NAMI Central Texas)*

"Mind Over Moment delivers incredible insights wrapped in truth served up with a healthy heaping of humor! Filled with practical, action-oriented takeaways based in research, this book is a must read for those who want to end the struggle of daily life and begin living their life to the fullest."

—*Colette Carlson, Founder of Speak Your Truth, Inc.*

MIND

OVER

MOMENT

HARNESS THE POWER OF RESILIENCE

ANNE GRADY

©2020 Anne Grady

www.annegradygroup.com

anne@annegradygroup.com

(512) 821-1111

PO Box 5815

Round Rock, TX 78683

Edited by Phyllis Jask

Cover design and text by Brenda Hawkes

Author photos by Jay Grady

Printed in the United States of America

ISBN-13: 979-8670043847

Jay, Rylee, and Evan
Thank you for so many delicious moments.
I love you.

CONTENTS

PREFACE: HAPPILY EVER, AFTER xi

GRATITUDES xv

INTRODUCTION xvii

PART ONE: MINDSET 1

Mind Over Moment 3

The Art (and Science) of Resilience 4

The Struggle Is Real 5

Make Friends with Your Brain 7

Overcome Your Negativity Bias 10

Get to Know Your Habits 14

Shift Your Mental Habits 17

Reconsider Your Story 18

Get to Know Your Mindset 21

You Are Not Helpless 24

Take Back Control 26

Break Out of Reactivity 28

Your Relationship with Stress 30

Beat Burnout 32

Change Your View of Stress 34

Transform Your Stress Response 36

Rethink "Busy" 38

Be Where You Are When You're There 39

Stop Multitasking 41

Take Control of Digital Distractions 42

Resilience Requires Courage 44

Resilience Takes Grit 45

Maximize Your Mindset 46

PART TWO: SKILLSET 47

Resilience and Emotional Intelligence 49

Grow Your Emotional Intelligence 50

Emotional Regulation 53

Get to Know Your Triggers.. 54

Manage Your Emotional Responses.................................. 55

Embrace Crappy Emotions 59

Proactively Cultivate Positive Emotions 62

Practice Optimism.. 63

Choose Gratitude... 67

Savor Delicious Moments 68

Build a Gratitude Habit 71

Find Humor... 73

Practice Mindfulness.. 76

Train Your Brain with Meditation 79

Be Compassionate Toward Yourself................................. 82

Be Compassionate Toward Others 85

Make Time for Social Connection 86

Hope Is a Strategy 89

Get a Helper's High.. 90

Take Care of Your Most Valuable Resource 93

Exercise Works 94

Sweet Dreams 96

Toot Your Horn 98

Practice Strategic Stopping... 99

Develop Your Skillset.. 100

PART 3: RESET 101

    Swim Toward Your Lighthouse 103

    Pick Your Lighthouse 104

    Define Success 106

    Success Is a Habit 108

    Pay Attention to Your Priorities 110

    Work/Life Balance Is Not the Goal 112

    Stop Searching for Your Passion 115

    The Power of Purpose 118

    Embrace Fear and Failure 120

    Tame Your Fear 121

    Learn from Failure 122

    Fear of Not Measuring Up 124

    Vulnerability Makes Us Stronger 126

    Mental Health Lessons from the Trenches 128

    Incorporate Mind Over Moment Every Day 130

CONCLUSION 135

STRONG ENOUGH 137

ABOUT THE AUTHOR 139

NOTES 141

PREFACE: HAPPILY, EVER AFTER

When I read fairy tales as a kid, nowhere did they mention princes or princesses fighting over who loads the dishwasher, picks up the kids, or pays the bills. There was no mention of high cholesterol, anti-depressants, or gluten-free diets. These stories all ended with one line... *and they lived happily ever after.* Happily, ever after? What does that even mean?

I was all teed up for this "happily ever after" life I'd read about. I am goal-oriented and have had a strategic plan for my life since I was a freshman in high school. No, I was not one of the popular kids. I was the president of my debate team and took theater arts. I was *that* kid. By the time I was in college, I thought I had it pretty dialed in. I was going to find Prince Charming and marry him at the age of 26, have my first child at 28, and my second child at 32. I was going to have dogs. Cute ones. I wanted a nice home with a white picket fence in a beautiful neighborhood. I thought I was doing everything right. I went to college, got a master's degree, got married at 26, had my first child at 28. I had mastered adulting.

In my TEDx talks and first two books, I went into painful details about my son Evan, who suffers with severe mental illness and autism. Long story short, I knew something wasn't right when Evan was born. Take the crankiest baby you have ever met and add an extra helping of cranky. That was Evan. Evan's father left when Evan was 18 months old (apparently Prince Charming wasn't so charming), leaving me to figure out how to navigate a new consulting career, a special needs child, and this whole "happily ever after" thing.

Evan is an incredible kid, and I love him more than I ever thought I could love another human. He is handsome, well-spoken, loving, and funny. He is also neuro-atypical and has a diagnosis of autism, a severe mood disorder, learning disabilities, oppositional defiant disorder, sensory integration processing disorder, and a partridge in a pear tree. His brain is a perfect neurological storm.

After several years of being a single mom, I remarried an incredible man and was blessed with his beautiful daughter Rylee. Jay is one of the best things to ever happen in my life. He is my partner, both personally and professionally, he is my best friend, and he is the most incredible father I've ever met. Not only did he embrace us with open arms, he became a father to Evan and loves him as his own. Rylee was five when I met her, and that little girl has changed my life. I'm so grateful to get to be her mom. She has endured her share of trauma, but she is a shining example of strength, courage, and resilience.

Evan was seven years old the first time he was hospitalized. While he was in the pediatric psych unit of Children's Medical Center in Dallas, Jay and I lived at the Ronald McDonald House for two months. At 10 years old, Evan was hospitalized again, and around the same time, I was diagnosed with a tumor in my salivary gland that resulted in facial paralysis, a scratched cornea, eye surgery, and radiation—but not before falling down a flight of stairs, breaking my foot in four places. And if you've heard me speak, this is where I say, "You can't make this shit up!"

We are taught that if we behave well, make good choices, and do the right things, that there is some elusive happy place where we are all supposed to end up. Then we grow up, lose a job, get a divorce, have a sick kid, or experience any number of other normal things, and suddenly, that "happily ever after" has burst into flames. It's easy to get discouraged. It's easy to throw up our hands and say, "Well, I guess this is just life." It's easy to settle for the life we have ended up with rather than create the one we deserve. Here's the thing, though: easy doesn't get us where we want to go, and easy comes with a price.

As I write this, Evan is 17 years old. When he was 15, we made the gut-wrenching decision to place him in a therapeutic boarding school in Idaho. It was by far the hardest decision we have ever had to make, but it was the right one. We could not give him the kind of immersive and intensive therapy he needed. We could not take breaks after a six- or eight-hour shift and tap out, and we couldn't manage the outbursts, aggression, and chaos that had become our life. His doctor put it quite simply: Either continue the way you are and ruin your marriage, your family, and your health, or save your family and save Evan in the process. When it was put it like that, things became crystal clear.

Although we see Evan every month, talk almost daily, and have weekly therapy video calls, we have had a much-needed break, and the respite has been profound. It has given us the time and space to take a step back, breathe, and gain some perspective. Through our own therapy, we have learned how we can be more empathetic and supportive, and we have become better parents and people because of it.

Evan has asked that I share his story because he wants to help other people know they are not alone, he wants to reduce the stigma of mental illness, and he knows what an impact this message can have on others. His willingness to be vulnerable to help people may very well be my proudest accomplishment. While I share some of our most challenging experiences, know that there are just as many amazing moments. Evan is making incredible progress, and I am beyond proud of the young man he has become.

Through chaos, I found clarity. I could continue to repeat the same cycle and end up where I was headed, or I could live on purpose, altering my path and crafting the life I want and deserve. I chose the latter. Now I'm here to help you do the same.

GRATITUDES

I am beyond grateful for the special people in my life. I cannot imagine being on this journey without you.

Jay, you are my best friend, my business partner, and the absolute love of my life. Thank you for your love, laughter, gentle nudges, and for believing in me. There is no one I'd rather be stuck on an island with.

Rylee, I am so proud of the woman you have become. You are a shining example of courage and strength, and I am so grateful to get to be your mom.

Evan, your bravery in allowing me to share your story makes my heart smile. Thank you for teaching me how to love unconditionally. I love you up to God and back.

Mom, thank you for being here every step of the way. Your love, encouragement, and endless support have inspired me to keep going and never give up hope.

Chuck and my Dads, thank you for teaching me strength and giving me the confidence that I can be anything I put my mind to.

To my AGG family, I could not have done this without you. Jay, thanks for being my VP of Everything. You are my bestie, and I love you. Deena, thank you for being my right arm and for your love, loyalty, and constant support. Amy, thank you for your creativity, encouragement, kindness, and laughter. Mind Over Moment was born because of you. And to the rest of the courageous and resilient AGG gang, you are the Tootsie to my roll. Thank you for helping me share these messages with the world.

Phyllis and Brenda, thank you for bringing my books to life and for helping me to tell my story. I am forever grateful.

To my beautiful friends and family, my mom has always told me that if you are blessed enough to have a handful of close friendships in your life, it has been a life well lived. I'm going to need more hands. Thank you for being a source of love, light, laughter, and strength. I am a better person because of you.

To those who have courageously shared their stories with me over the years, you have inspired me. Thank you for your prayers, love, laughs, and support. I am forever grateful.

And to you, yes you. Life is short. Live yours on purpose.

Introduction

When I was little, I had a gerbil named Penelope. I really wanted a puppy, but after the unfortunate guinea pig incident of 1981, a gerbil was the best I was going to get. In 1981, I was six years old, and my dad had the brilliant idea to get me two guinea pigs, Wendy and John. Apparently, no one told him what happens when two guinea pigs fall in love. Needless to say, a short time later, we had no shortage of guinea pigs—within a few months, there were *20*. After said incident, we had 19. How can a six-year-old keep track of 20 guinea pigs? Suffice it to say, I was lucky to get Penelope.

At first, having a gerbil was adorable. After about a week, she got annoying. She ran on her gerbil wheel for hours never going anywhere. She would eat and then run on the wheel. Sleep and run on the wheel. Look up and run on the wheel. You get the picture. That little gerbil got her steps in every single day, but she went absolutely nowhere.

I can't pinpoint the exact time, but sometime in my mid-30s, I had become Penelope. It seemed like I was always running, metaphorically speaking (I have two titanium pins in my left foot—Jimmy Buffet concert, coconut bra, long story—so running is not an option). I was always busy. I would wake up and run on my wheel, go to work and run on my wheel, come home and run on my wheel. I was very busy running on my wheel, but I was getting nowhere.

I see so many people struggling with what I call "The Penelope Syndrome." We wake up, check our phones, go to work, check our phones, react our way through the insanity that is our inbox, check our phones, stay busy, check our phones, sleep, and do it all over again. Some days are great, some days are crappy, and most are somewhere in between. But are we getting anywhere, or are we just running in circles?

If you can't relate because you have a perfect life and have all your shit together, go away. Nobody likes you. (Kidding!) But if you have ever felt like me—just surviving each day, barely hanging on until weekends, doing your best to keep commitments yet often feeling like you're falling short—keep reading because, baby, this book is for you!

I have developed an approach, along with a set of tools and strategies to help get and keep you off the gerbil wheel. Some of these skills are a continuation of those I wrote about in my first two books, *52 Strategies for Life, Love & Work: Transforming Your Life One Week at a Time* and *Strong Enough: Choosing Courage, Resilience, and Triumph*. I've been using them most of my adult life and have grown and adapted them along the way.

As I write this book, the world is battling the COVID-19 pandemic, and it's turned us all sideways. Far too many of us are struggling with crippling anxiety stemming from very real concerns: our health, the health of our loved ones, our finances, the economy, our kids' education—there's no shortage of stress to occupy our every waking moment. It is in times like these that the strategies in these pages are put to the test. They have been my lifeline. Whether you are navigating a pandemic or life in general, my hope is that this book will provide practical tools to help make that journey a little easier.

Mind Over Moment is a science-based approach that uses mindfulness to help you strengthen your resilience, emotional intelligence, health, and relationships. Thousands of scientific studies have documented the physical, mental, and emotional benefits of practicing mindfulness—lower blood pressure, better sleep, improved mood, stronger relationships, and reduction in stress, anxiety, and depression, just to name a few. Mind Over Moment is a collection of tools to help you become aware of your thoughts, feelings, habits, and behaviors in the moment, in order to steer yourself toward better responses and outcomes.

The practice of Mind Over Moment is just that—a practice. None of us are perfect, and we are not going to get everything right all the time. We are all a work in progress. When we practice these habits, beliefs, and behaviors, we empower ourselves to get beyond the moments that urgently trigger our brains to react; we allow ourselves to stop, take charge of our thoughts, and reroute our fight-or-flight way of thinking. We can train our minds to be resilient. I use these skills every day because, let's face it, life is unpredictable at best, and I want to do whatever I can to get that extra push to get through the challenging and messy stuff.

I've divided this book into three parts, each one covering the whats, hows, and whys of practicing Mind Over Moment.

Part One explores the toolbox we all have—our mindset. Building resilience starts with your belief system because your beliefs drive your behavior. Part Two delves into the tools themselves—specific strategies to help you practice Mind Over Moment. Part Three covers the reset—your ability to step outside of reactivity and create the life you truly deserve.

Throughout the book, I share my personal experiences using Mind Over Moment. These practices have helped to transform my life, and I am confident they will do the same for you. To make the most out of these strategies, check out the accompanying Mind Over Moment journal. *Mind Over Moment Journal: Simple Reminders to Harness the Power of Resilience* is filled with prompts, thought-provoking questions, and personal exploration exercises to help transfer learning into real life.

Part One:
MINDSET

Resilience is a set of beliefs, skills, and habits that you can proactively develop and build, just like a muscle. Your ability to build resilience is based on your mindset, your skill set, and your ability to reset. Let's start with your mindset.

Think of your mindset as a toolbox. It is your foundation and the place where your new skills, habits, and behaviors are stored. Your habits and belief system impact the way you see yourself, interact with those around you, view adversity, and so much more. What we practice grows stronger, both positively and negatively. Practicing a resilient mindset begins with identifying, recognizing, and acknowledging habits and beliefs that drive your behavior. Much of your life is based on habits. Mind Over Moment means being deliberate about cultivating the right ones.

MIND OVER MOMENT

We are currently in a time unlike anything we have ever experienced. COVID-19 (coronavirus) is running rampant throughout the world, there are riots in the streets, and the level of civil unrest is unprecedented. Uncertainty, anxiety, and stress have become the new normal. News outlets with ominous music and "breaking stories" provide updates on this dire situation. Many areas, including mine in Austin, Texas, have been ordered to shelter in place. All non-essential travel, errands, or activities have been banned to curb the spread of this virus. The shit has hit the fan.

We have all just been given an unimaginable opportunity to build resilience. Whether it is in this time of crisis or in your normal world, life has become increasingly complicated. There are no simple solutions to the frenetic pace of life today. You will always have to juggle work, family, health, finances, and the other dozen things on your plate. And although you cannot always control the chaos, you can control how you respond to it by shifting your mindset to purposely respond rather than react.

Mind Over Moment is a practice to help you do just that. It's a drawer of mental tools to help you recalibrate your thoughts, feelings, habits, and behaviors in the moments you have them so you can better control your responses and outcomes.

Most of us react through life directionless and end up where we are headed. Mind Over Moment means paying attention—in each moment—to decisions you are otherwise making unwittingly so you can create the life you truly deserve. It's about stopping to ask "Is the way I am thinking and behaving going to get me the result I want? Or am I willing to settle for the result I am getting based on how I am thinking and behaving?" It's either one or the other.

Mind Over Moment is about being proactive and deliberate in the choices you make and the habits you practice, throughout your day, week, month, and life. It is becoming aware of the thoughts and beliefs that drive your behavior so you can identify whether those beliefs are serving you. Mind Over Moment means choosing what you want your life to look like so you can create a path to get there. Most importantly, it is about breaking out of reactivity so you can live your life on purpose. This is a practice, and there is no perfect. All you can do is take one day at a time, giving yourself grace to do the best you can, and forgiving yourself when you fall short. All you can do is all you can do (that's one of my favorite mantras).

"Mind Over Moment means choosing what you want your life to look like so you can create a path to get there."

Life is full of twists and turns, and there will be times when you have no other choice but to react. That's why it's so important to take control of the times you can.

THE ART (AND SCIENCE) OF RESILIENCE

Resilience is your ability to bounce back from adversity, but it is also much more. Resilience allows you to tap into your own strength and courage so you can pivot when things don't go as you had planned. When you are resilient, you have the stores of energy, creativity, problem-solving, and emotional intelligence that you need to navigate everything life throws at you. Resilient people excel in problem solving, positive communication, emotional intelligence, and emotional regulation; are more hopeful and optimistic; and have higher levels of self-esteem.

Just like any other muscle, you must devote time and energy to build resilience. Regardless of how many times you've been knocked down, the fact that you are reading this means you are, by your very nature, resilient. Life gives you plenty of chances to practice; each time you overcome a challenge you are using your hard-earned skills to propel yourself forward—smarter and stronger.

The Struggle Is Real

What makes some people go through difficult times and crumble, yet others get stronger? I couldn't get this question out of my head. People told me I was brave. I certainly didn't feel that way. I was terrified. People told me I was resilient, but I felt broken. And people told me I was strong, but I honestly didn't feel strong enough. Yet despite my lack of belief in my own courage, resilience, and strength, *I was still standing.* No matter how exhausted I was, how hopeless I felt, and how worn down I had become, the sun continued to rise.

You have survived the worst things that have ever happened to you. You have lost loved ones, had your heart broken, experienced trauma, and had a stomach bug or food poisoning that you prayed would kill you just to stop your misery. Everyone goes through their share of crud, and nobody gets out of this life unscathed. If you're thinking, "I have challenges, but my situation is nothing compared to so and so's," I'm here to tell you not to waste your time comparing your suffering to someone else's. We all struggle at 100 percent. It's all relative, and whatever's going on with you is real to you. Struggle is not a competition.

"Struggle is not a competition."

After sharing my story in speeches, people come up to me and share theirs. There was a young man in his 30s who had had multiple brain surgeries—losing his sight and hearing in the process—but he kept a smile on his face and had a great sense of humor. One woman had her home ruined by Hurricane Katrina, only to have her next house burn down in the California wildfires. A woman hugged me a couple of months ago and started to sob. She had been diagnosed with Stage IV breast cancer the week before and had recently lost her husband. A few months ago, I attended the funeral of my dear friend's daughter. She was 26 years old.

After talking with hundreds of people who have gone through unspeakable experiences, I found a common thread. The one thing these people have in common is the belief that they are stronger and more resilient as a result. Did they want to endure this crap? Absolutely not. But in doing so, they have become smarter and stronger for it.

I started to get even more curious. Are there things you can do to build resilience before you need it so that you don't have to wait until adversity strikes? Can you proactively build your resilience muscle? The research is clear, and the answer is a resounding yes. And just like any other muscle, you have to take it to its limits before it grows stronger. There is no growth without discomfort.

Resilience is neither a fixed trait nor is it something some of us are just lucky to have. Resilience is a set of habits, skills, and behaviors that can be proactively cultivated and practiced.

"There is no growth without discomfort."

Building resilience requires you to be deliberate about the choices you make, the habits you practice, and the skills you build so that you can step out of reactivity and take back control of your life. You wouldn't enter a marathon without training. Now it's time to train for the stuff that will inevitably happen, so that when it does, you are able to rise to the challenge.

The research is clear—resilience is not just an art but a science.[1] There are both tactical and strategic approaches to build resilience and evidence-based practices that will grow your resilience muscle. It is an art because no two people's journeys are alike, and the strategies that may work for one person may be different than what works for the next. Resilience is abstract, messy, and almost never built when everything is peachy. Fortunately, there are scientifically proven ways to build your resilience muscle to give you the strength to persevere when you need it the most. We'll get into those strategies in Part Two.

MAKE FRIENDS WITH YOUR BRAIN

Life is full of emotional and stressful situations. How you respond to those situations as they arise has a profound effect on your productivity, relationships, and health, and it all starts with that melon sitting on top of your shoulders.

I am not a neuroscientist, but I have been studying the brain since Evan was born, talking to neurologists, psychiatrists, neuropsychologists, and just about any healthcare professional I could find. Here is what I've learned:

The human brain has gone through three levels of evolution. The first level of evolution is our reptilian brain. This primitive part of the brain is responsible for heart rate, breathing, respiration, and balance. Basically, it controls things we don't even think about.

The next evolution is our limbic system. This is the part of the brain responsible for our emotions, memories, and habits. It is the emotional cockpit of the brain. It's also home to the amygdala, an almond-shaped set of neurons and grey matter deep in the brain's medial temporal lobe. These little guys trigger our fight-or-flight response.

The most recent evolution, the neocortex, surrounds the outer part of the brain. The prefrontal cortex, right behind our forehead, is the part of the brain that is responsible for higher level thinking, problem solving, attention management, decision making, emotional regulation, creativity and so much more.

Your brain is complex and amazing. It is more powerful than the world's fastest supercomputer and is capable of so much more than you can even begin to imagine. It can also be your greatest enemy. Your brain processes thousands of thoughts each day, most of which are repetitive and negative. Breaking news! Layoffs! A free fall in our economy! Death! We are bombarded with negative messages. Our brains go on high alert scanning for threats waiting to pounce. It's like a police speed trap, and you are going 120mph in a school zone. Whether we realize it or not, we are priming our brains to seek out more threats, negative information, and worst-case scenarios. Those negative thoughts once served a purpose and helped protect our ancestors when they were on the lookout for threats like saber-tooth tigers.

Unfortunately, your brain doesn't differentiate between a real threat and a perceived threat. Your brain doesn't know the difference between a tiger or a snarky email from your boss.

Let's imagine you are walking through a beautiful field of flowers. Suddenly, a tiger lunges toward you. If you are lucky enough to survive, you are more likely to remember the tiger than the beautiful flowers because, let's face it, the flowers were not going to eat you!

Your brain deeply encodes negative experiences into your neural network to protect you. It's called a "negativity bias." Your focus on the negative is an evolutionary response engrained from a time when survival depended upon being constantly on the lookout for threats. Despite human evolution, your brain continues to overestimate threats and underestimate opportunities as a result of this survival mechanism.

Your negativity bias may protect you, but it can also play dirty tricks on your brain. For example, let's say you get a performance review and are told you've done nine things exceptionally well, but you have one "opportunity for growth." When you are lying in bed at night, it's the "opportunity for growth" that occupies most of your headspace, not the nine things you did well.

> "Your negativity bias may protect you, but it can also play dirty tricks on your brain."

After many conferences or training sessions, I get evaluations from people who attended. A huge percentage of the evaluations are overwhelmingly positive, but you can't please everyone all the time.

After a big conference I got an evaluation that said, "No one wants to hear you talk about your kid or your problems." At first, it crushed me. I thought about it before I went to sleep, after I woke up, and several times throughout the next couple of days. I realized that I had let this one comment take up way too much valuable real estate in my brain. Then, I practiced Mind Over Moment to catch myself: I purposely recognized the feelings and thoughts, sat with them for a moment, acknowledged that it was just one person's opinion, and moved on.

Unfortunately, the propensity to lean toward the negative makes it easier to skip over the good stuff in life and magnify the bad stuff. So, although you might remember a delicious meal, you don't give it the same time and attention as you would the fire alarm that went off in the restaurant while you were eating it.

The problem is that when you ruminate on the negative, you etch negativity deeper into your mind map, making you spend much of your time anxious, on alert, and unable to relax. This makes you more prone to look for and find the negative. See the cycle? If you are not careful, this becomes your default way of thinking.

Your brain encodes negative experiences immediately to protect you and keep you safe. Unfortunately, positive experiences take a little longer to marinate before they are embedded deeply into your neural mind map.

When you spend your time ruminating on the negative, lying in bed at night thinking "I could have...should have...wish I would have...," you increase the likelihood that you will continue to think that way. When was the last time something good happened and you just savored it? You visualized it, meditated on it, and fell asleep thinking about it? Chances are that those nights don't happen as frequently.

> *"When was the last time something good happened and you just savored it?"*

You can see examples of this in everyday interactions. For example, have you ever debated a compliment? I was speaking at an event and afterward a woman said to me, "Oh, I like your shoes." My response: "These? I got these at Marshall's for 20 bucks." Instead of saying thank you and appreciating the time she took to give me a compliment, I dismissed it and moved on. Not only did I miss an opportunity to embed a positive memory, I turned it into a negative. Score a point for the negative noggin.

Or what about "I'm sorry"? How many times a day do you say those two words? When you say it habitually, you send a message to your brain that you are less than. When you habitually say you are sorry, you are telling yourself and others that you are responsible for problems even when you bear no responsibility. According to some psychologists, over-apologizing may also be a sign of anxiety. If you listen intently, you'll see that women are way worse about this than men. If a man bumps into someone, he's likely to say, "excuse me," or "pardon me." When women bump into people, we are more likely to say, "I'm sorry." I catch myself saying it all the time. Start your own "I'm sorry" counter and pay attention to how often you say it.

If you allow your negativity bias to get stronger, you will operate out of a place of fear and anxiety. This shrinks your short-term memory, making it more difficult for you to focus and regulate your emotions.

OVERCOME YOUR NEGATIVITY BIAS

Fortunately, you can break out of habits like over-apologizing and ruminating on negative thoughts and feelings. Through something called "experience-dependent neuroplasticity," you can remap your brain and make it easier to find the good stuff.

Your brain is malleable and changes based on your experiences, thoughts, and behaviors. Experience-dependent neuroplasticity is the brain's ability to create new neural pathways based on new experiences. Basically, the more you think and behave a certain way, the easier it is to think and behave that way. When you look for reasons to be grateful, or look for the positive in people and situations, the very act of looking increases serotonin and dopamine, neurotransmitters that trigger positive emotions, as well as reduce the stress hormone cortisol. You feel better, and you can respond rather than react. When you look for the negative, you find that as well, setting off a completely different neurochemical chain reaction.[2]

"Experience-dependent neuroplasticity is the brain's ability to create new neural pathways based on new experiences."

You can change your brain if you spend more time magnifying the positive in your life and less time worrying about what you can't control or ruminating on the negative. For instance, next time you are lying in bed at night and your mind gravitates toward negative thoughts, just observe those thoughts and watch them float by like a cloud. Thoughts aren't good or bad, so no judgment is needed. I catch myself having negative thoughts and then scolding myself for thinking that way. That only exacerbates the problem. Thoughts and emotions are simply information. Once you observe them objectively, you can choose whether or not you engage them. We are often taught to replace a negative thought with a positive one. Supportive phrases like "turn that frown upside down" are actually not that supportive. Your brain can't make that leap from one end of the emotional continuum to the other, so it starts debating the new thought and pretty soon, you are in a boxing match with yourself.

If you have ever tried to just stop thinking negative thoughts, you know that it doesn't work. Whatever you do as you read this, do not think about pink elephants. I repeat, do not think about pink elephants. Do not think about cute, baby, big-eared, tutu wearing, pink elephants. So, what did you think about? Your mind inevitably goes to the thing I told you not to think about. Trying to stop thinking about something makes you more likely to think about it. This is the reason diets don't work. Don't think about chocolate cake. Don't think about pizza or that juicy cheeseburger. Don't think about chips and queso. And whatever you do, do not think about tacos! You get the point. And how can you not think about tacos?

In order to reduce negative thoughts associated with anxiety, stress, and depression, you have a couple of options. I find it most effective to combine the two. The first is through practicing mindfulness, which is the basis for Mind Over Moment. This simply means giving yourself the time and space to feel what you're feeling, knowing that it is temporary. Thoughts or feelings are neither good nor bad, and they are fleeting. Pay attention to the sensations in your body. Do you feel tension in your stomach? Have your shoulders tightened? Then watch the thought float by like a cloud on a breezy day. The goal is simply to bring yourself back to the present moment. You can choose to engage thoughts and feelings, but you can also choose not to.

As someone who has struggled my whole life with what are called ANTs (Automatic Negative Thoughts), this has been profound for me. Mind Over Moment means I don't have to constantly debate my thoughts but just recognize them, observe them nonjudgmentally, and let them pass. This takes their power away, and repeated practice creates a habit.

"You can choose to engage thoughts and feelings, but you can also choose not to."

I'm someone who wants to solve problems and "fix" things; it has been an eye-opening experience learning to sit with those feelings and thoughts, observing them, without judgment.

The second approach is to challenge the validity of those thoughts and replace them with more productive ones so that you can cultivate positive emotions instead. This is the basis for cognitive behavioral therapy. The key is to identify underlying thought patterns, challenge them, and reshape them to be more productive.

For example, if you make a mistake in a meeting or on a project, it is very easy to slip into negative self-talk, convincing yourself that you are stupid, careless, or inept. You can challenge that thought, realizing that it is not the truth, and that there are plenty of times you say and do the right thing. Then you can replace that thought with something like, "I made a mistake, and I'm human. I will get it right the next time." I've found you must first learn to recognize the thought, get curious about it, and experience it. Then you can challenge the validity.

As the coronavirus has swept through the world, the level of anxiety and depression has sky-rocketed, and people are operating out of a place of fear. I own a small business and felt my own anxiety rise as I watched one speaking engagement after another get postponed or canceled altogether. I had a choice. I could stay in a place of fear, wondering how I will support my team and my family, or I could practice Mind Over Moment.

Instead of trying to push those feelings away, I simply observe them. When I take a moment to breathe, I realize I'm wearing my shoulders as earrings, my stomach has tightened, and my foot is bouncing my leg up and down. I observe, notice the emotion, notice the feeling, and then bring myself back to this moment because in this moment, I am safe.

"Instead of pushing feelings away, simply observe them."

Then, I move into challenging some of the self-defeating thoughts. In total transparency, here is where my head naturally goes:

What if I lose my income? What if I let my team down? We won't be able to get Evan the help he needs. He'll get worse! He'll be homeless! We'll be homeless! What if we can't pay for Rylee's college or her housing! Run! The zombies are chasing me!

Not only are these thoughts not true, they are not helpful. By simply observing the way I'm thinking and feeling, I have taken back control and have gone from my emotional brain to my logical brain. This allows me to see the situation objectively without getting carried away by it. Now is the chance to re-write the narrative in my head. Here is the more realistic thought:

I have built a successful business from the ground up despite incredible odds. I have demonstrated strength, resilience, and resourcefulness. My team is amazing and has stepped up above and beyond. We are smart, and we will figure this out.

Our beliefs are powerful because beliefs drive behavior. Fortunately, beliefs can be changed just like any other habit.

Get to Know Your Habits

The Greek lyrical poet Archilochus once said, "We don't rise to the level of our expectations, we fall to the level of our training." Take that a step further. You don't rise to the level of your intentions, you fall to the level of your habits.

When you are stressed, tired, or under pressure, you are more likely to fall back on habitual patterns of thinking and behaving. But do those habits serve you? Will they help you create the life you want?

"You don't rise to the level of your intentions, you fall to the level of your habits."

Your brain loves habits because it doesn't have to work as hard. Even negative habits are more comfortable than new ones. Once you start recognizing patterns, you can make intentional choices about the habits you choose to maintain and adopt. This is the basis of Mind Over Moment.

A habit is something that once required conscious effort but has become automatic. It turns out, a large portion of what you do each day is a habit. In fact, more than 45 percent of what you do every single day is a habit.[3] Your brain depends on these cognitive shortcuts to conserve energy. If you have ever driven home on autopilot because you were deep in thought, you were operating out of habit.

You live almost half your life on autopilot. If you are not careful, you can become a slave to your habits, and they can become a way to live life unconsciously, rather than deliberately choosing what you want and creating a path to get there.

> *"If you are not careful, you can become a slave to your habits."*

Habits can be super helpful. After all, if you had to think really hard about putting on shoes, eating, taking a shower, or getting dressed, you would be exhausted by 9:00 am. Your habits allow you to conserve mental energy.

Have you ever been to the grocery store after they have rearranged the shelves? For the love of Pete, where'd they put the peanut butter? Why is it so exhausting hunting for items you used to know were on aisle 11? Even without realizing it, when you plan your trip to the store, you visualize what you need in each of the aisles because you know where things are. Your brain has a map, basically a neural network that gets more deeply etched the more you think or do something. This makes it much easier to think or do the things you have always thought and done.

During the coronavirus crisis, trips to the store have been increasingly difficult. People are hoarding cleaning supplies, canned food, paper products, and more. I still can't understand why it's impossible to find toilet paper. It's not a stomach virus! Walking in the store yesterday was bizarre. Aisles formerly stocked ceiling-high were empty. The brands and products I typically buy were gone. I found myself disoriented, not familiar with the aisles when they weren't organized as they had been before. We depend on habits.

Unfortunately, your brain doesn't know the difference between a good habit and a bad habit. It doesn't know the difference between being anxious, worried, and fearful or optimistic, excited, and grateful. It doesn't know the difference between getting home from work and drinking a bottle of wine or going to the gym. Your brain just takes anything you repeatedly think, say, or do, and converts it into a habit.

Take a second to try something. Cross your arms like you are cold or angry. Now cross them in the opposite direction. Which way feels more awkward? When you crossed your arms the first time, the signal came from your limbic system. It's a habit—you've done it a million times, and you didn't even have to think about it. The second time you crossed your arms, the signal came from your prefrontal cortex. It was probably a little odd, clunky, and uncomfortable, and you had to think about it. If you practice crossing your arms in that direction regularly, eventually that will become a habit too.

Building resilience requires that you be deliberate about your habits. It means you must challenge your automatic thoughts and behaviors, and that is hard work. When it comes to your life, personally and professionally, what habits are supporting your success, and which habits are sabotaging it?

There is no timetable for habit change. Your neuropathways have been carved deeply, and it takes repetitive, consistent change to build new neuropathways. And just because you develop a new neuropathway does not mean old ones are erased—which means it's easy to slip back into old habit patterns.

"When it comes to your life, personally and professionally, what habits are supporting your success, and which habits are sabotaging it?"

Think of your brain like a field full of grass. You can walk through the field, but the grass will still pop back up. You may have to walk in the exact place a hundred times before a pathway is carved. And just because you carve new pathways doesn't mean the old ones aren't still well-worn and comfortable. Old bumpy paths that we know can be more comfortable than the smooth ones we don't. To change habit patterns, you have to be willing to get comfortable being uncomfortable.

SHIFT YOUR MENTAL HABITS

If I let my mind go where it wants to naturally, I am likely to ruminate on the negative. I second guess myself, question my own decisions, and regret things I've said or didn't say. I should have…I could have…I wish I would have. I could spend all day "shoulding" on myself if I'm not careful. It has become a habit, and it is one I'm working to change. Practicing Mind Over Moment means that I catch myself while it's happening and make a conscious decision about what to do next.

Unfortunately, you can't just break a habit, but you can replace an unproductive thought with a more productive one. Notice I didn't say a positive one. Your brain can't make the jump from, "I can't believe I said that!" to "I'm so happy I said that!" It can, however, go from a negative thought to a realistic one. It can go from, "I can't believe I said that!" to "It is what it is. Move on."

Is this easy? No! This stuff isn't for sissies. Word of caution: Do *not* try to change multiple habits at once. It's a recipe for failure. Think about New Year's resolutions. You have made a pact with yourself. This year is going to be different. You're going to eat better, work out more, and drink less. By January 15th, you have a beer in one hand and a cheeseburger in the other. You went to the gym. That hurt! Why would you do that again? And then you revert right back to old behavior.

In his book *Habit Stacking*, S.J. Scott introduces the concept of combining habits to help you adopt a new behavior. Because new habits are difficult to cultivate, he suggests "stacking" a new habit onto an existing one. For example, you brush your teeth every day (hopefully even twice a day). If you are trying to build a habit of practicing gratitude, pick a time, either right before or right after you brush your teeth.

Then think of three specific things you are grateful for. This morning mine were:

- I am grateful my family and friends are healthy.
- I am grateful that I have plenty of food, water, and a beautiful shelter.
- I am grateful the weather was nice so I could take a walk this morning.

Adding a new habit to an existing one makes it easier to stick with it.

Behavior change happens one of three ways: Rarely, slowly, or never. In *52 Strategies for Life, Love and Work,* I wrote about the slight edge. It's not the big changes made all at once that change a habit. It's the little things, done repeatedly and over time that create new behaviors and thought patterns.

> *"It's not the big changes made all at once that change a habit. It's the little things, done repeatedly and over time that create new behaviors and thought patterns."*

RECONSIDER YOUR STORY

Do you talk to yourself? Some of you just said "yes" out loud. The rest of you are sitting there with your finger over your mouth quietly muttering, "Do I talk to myself?" Yes, you do, and you listen to yourself as well. Your mindset is built by the stories you tell yourself about yourself, and those stories determine how you live your life. It turns out that many of the stories you've been telling yourself about yourself are just plain wrong.

I told myself story after story about my ability as a mom. None of the doctors could explain what was happening with Evan, and a few even suggested it was my parenting ability. This narrative permeated every aspect of my life. Being a mom was my most important job.

I felt like I was failing miserably. Nothing would work. How could I help others if I couldn't even parent my child? Was I going to screw up Rylee, just like I did Evan? I felt total shame.

It's difficult to see the world in a way that is inconsistent with the way you see yourself. If you're sending yourself messages like "I'm not good enough" and "I'm unhappy," you will start to believe those things because you find what you look for. It's called "selective attention."

Selective attention means your brain subconsciously filters out some things while focusing in on others. Your brain directs attention to things that match what is already top of mind. It's why when you're in a bad mood, things come through that filter, and you are more likely to find the negative. Every traffic light seems to turn red, people are annoying, and everything that can go wrong seems to.

> *"Your brain directs attention to things that match what is already top of mind."*

I found myself comparing Evan to other people's kids, and my parenting skills to that of my friends. Every time Evan had a meltdown (which was usually several times a day), I beat myself up. One morning, we were driving on the highway. Evan was four years old, and he was in the backseat having a fit because he didn't want to be in his booster seat. He was screaming at me as I was going 70mph down a busy highway, and there was nowhere to pull over. I looked back, and Evan had gotten out of his seat, opened the car door, and threatened to jump.

After almost getting into an accident, I was finally able to exit and slow down, all while pleading with him not to jump. "I'll take you for ice cream! Would you like that? How about we go for ice cream?" Evan stopped crying and got back in his seat. We drove in silence to a local ice cream shop, both of us with tear-stained eyes. And then my "story" kicked in.

Why didn't I have the child locks on! What is wrong with me! I'm sure my friends don't forget the child locks. And I offered him ice cream?! No wonder he misbehaves, I give in and enable the behavior. What kind of mother would forget child locks and reward a tantrum with ice cream? I am a failure.

One of the most powerful things you can do to build resilience is to shift your mindset and your story.

Carol Dweck, a psychologist at Stanford, has pioneered research around just that. For over 40 years, Dweck has studied students' attitudes about learning and failure. She began by observing children working on puzzles. Some of the puzzles were extremely difficult and others were completely unsolvable. She found that while some students viewed failure as utter defeat, got frustrated, and gave up, others took it as a challenge and embraced it. In longitudinal studies, the students who embraced the idea of challenge, and even failure, had higher test scores, greater engagement, healthier relationships, and greater long-term success.[4]

Your mindset is a set of conscious or unconscious beliefs that affect how you think about your abilities, how you behave, and how you affect those around you. This view profoundly affects the way you live your life. Dweck found that what you believe about your ability to learn and grow is one of the key factors in how quickly you rebound from failure. Imagine your mindset is on a spectrum. On one end of the spectrum is a fixed mindset, and on the other end is a growth mindset. We all operate on this continuum every day. No one is either on one end of the spectrum or the other all the time. Different tasks, people, and circumstances may slide you in one direction or the other.

Take a moment to answer the following questions (honestly).

- Have you ever thought, "I'm just not a _____ person." (I'm just not a "math" person or, I'm not an "athletic" person.)

- Do you compare yourself to others? Have you ever wondered why a colleague got a promotion instead of you? After all, you work hard and deserve it.

- Have you ever found yourself not wanting to speak up because you're afraid you'll be judged or sound stupid?
- Do you get defensive when you receive negative feedback?

If you answered yes to these questions, as I initially did, you lean toward a fixed mindset.

GET TO KNOW YOUR MINDSET

Someone who operates with a fixed mindset believes that intelligence and ability are fixed. That although you can do things differently, the important parts of who you are can't really be changed. People who operate out of a fixed mindset try to prove themselves, to show that they are smart and talented, and when they make a mistake, they are worried about being judged or looking stupid. In my case, I felt like I was either a good mother or not. "Not" was the one I kept going with.

The growth mindset assumes that you can learn, grow, and improve no matter your age. When you adopt a growth mindset, it allows you to look at failure not as a blow to your self-esteem, but as a way to grow and improve. If you have a growth mindset, failure means you should try harder, stretch yourself, and continue to grow. It means you believe you are where you are, not because of some magical talent but because you work hard. If you take someone with raw talent who never works at something and someone with less talent who works hard, the person who works harder will prevail. Think Michael Jordan or Michael Phelps. Talent will only get you so far. These guys worked harder, trained more, and practiced relentlessly.

> "When you adopt a growth mindset, it allows you to look at failure not as a blow to your self-esteem, but as a way to grow and improve."

According to Dweck, people with a growth mindset don't necessarily believe they can do anything or be anything, but they do believe that with the proper education and preparation, they can continue to improve. Their mindset is, "Why waste my time proving myself when I could be learning something new?"

When babies learn to walk, they don't fall and think, "Well, I guess this walking thing just isn't for me!" They get up and keep trying. It's not until you get older and worry about what other people think that you slip into a fixed mindset.

Your brain does something differently when you are worried about failure and proving or protecting yourself than it does when you are focused on development, improvement, and growth. When you are worried about failure, your limbic system is engaged, your threat response kicks in, and your brain's main job is to protect you—your ego in this case. When you legitimately believe that failure is an inevitable part of the process, and your goal becomes to learn lessons from it and use those experiences to guide future goals, you are operating out of the prefrontal cortex, the part of the brain responsible for higher level thinking.

You constantly stretch yourself to learn new things, and when you inevitably fail, you use it as an opportunity to work harder and smarter. You use setbacks as valuable information to fine-tune your strategies moving forward. You believe that failure is only bad if you're perfect.

"Use setbacks as valuable information to fine-tune your strategies moving forward."

Dweck found women who struggle with failure are particularly vulnerable to a fixed mindset. When a woman fails, she is more likely to assign blame and criticism to her core self, rather than see the failure as a reflection of her effort or skills. When men take risks and miss the mark, they are often described as bold and brave. As women, we constantly judge ourselves. When we fail, we are more likely to see it as a reflection of our total worth and intelligence. Building your resilience muscle involves adopting new mindsets and better habits around how you face challenges. By increasing your willingness to feel the discomfort of uncertainty and failure, you can bounce back when things don't go as planned. You may have been conditioned to see failure as weakness. Those with growth mindsets can accept failure more readily because they view their traits as constantly under development.

Cultivating a growth mindset frees you from the shackles of believing your happiness is based on your intelligence or ability. When you base success on how hard you work, you can learn to view failure as a sign that you need to get better at a particular task.

"Cultivating a growth mindset frees you from the shackles of believing your happiness is based on your intelligence or ability."

When I read Dweck's book, I was surprised by my own fixed mindset. In addition to feeling like a bad mom, I also believed that I wasn't a math person or an athletic person. In the second grade after getting pegged in the face by a dodgeball, I declared myself "not an athletic person." And when my eighth-grade algebra teacher Mrs. Wilson made fun of me for asking too many questions, I just assumed I wasn't a "math person."

With a fixed mindset you compare yourself to others, wondering why they seem to catch all the breaks or move ahead faster. Someone with a growth mindset doesn't compare themselves to others. They are more focused on becoming better tomorrow than they were today. Why waste your time comparing yourself to others when you could spend that energy getting better?

The thing is, no one wants to look stupid. We naturally compare ourselves to others. And we gravitate toward tasks and subjects that are easy for us. The key is to be mindful, catching yourself shirking from a challenge because you are afraid to fail—and doing it anyway. Seeing challenges as opportunities allows you to proactively cultivate a growth mindset, and that can help you respond with resilience when life throws you a curveball. Your life is full of challenges and setbacks. When they happen, your mind interprets them differently based on your mindset.

The good news is that the way you think about learning changes the way you learn. As soon as I realized I was parenting with a fixed mindset, I moved into action. I started seeing therapists to learn behavioral strategies, I took classes, went to seminars, watched how my friends handled tantrums and misbehavior, and read every parenting book I could get my hands on.

Simply recognizing that you are slipping into a fixed mindset is enough to help you change it. Your mindset is nothing more than a set of beliefs, and *beliefs can be changed.*

You Are Not Helpless

How you deal with failure has everything to do with how you face obstacles and approach your goals. One sneaky mindset obstacle to beware of is called "learned helplessness."

Learned helplessness is the belief that things will be a certain way because they've always been that way before. Martin Seligman, commonly known as the founder of positive psychology, coined the term for the tendency to view outcomes as predetermined and uncontrollable. And we are not alone among species when it comes to believing in false limitations.

Elephants are some of the most majestic and powerful animals on the planet. In order to ensure they are compliant in captivity, trainers tie the leg of the baby elephant to a post. Regardless of how much it struggles, the baby cannot break free. As the elephant grows older and bigger, it has been conditioned to stay confined to the post, and even when it is strong enough to run away and take the post with it, the animal continues to believe it can't break free.

Something as small as a flea can learn to be helpless. Fleas can jump incredibly far for their small size. If you place a flea in a jar, you'd better close the lid fast, or it will jump out. Once you put the lid on, the flea learns to jump lower so it doesn't hit the lid. Eventually, if you take the lid off, the flea will no longer jump out of the jar.

Just like elephants and fleas, you can learn helplessness. You fail at something and then tell yourself a story of how you just can't do it. Started a business and failed? I'm just not an entrepreneur. Tried to create a band and failed? It's just not meant to be. Fell in love and got hurt? Relationships just aren't my thing. If you're not careful, you will believe the story you tell yourself about yourself.

Although it might not be a physical restraint like a tether to a pole or a lid on a jar, your fear of failure and your self-limiting beliefs create imaginary barriers you are convinced you can't break through.

One of the most powerful things you can do to build resilience is to shift your mindset and tell yourself a new story. Are you growing and getting better? If you are not willing to fail, the answer is no. Accept failure as part of the learning process but notice *how* you're failing. Use the failure as information, not judgment. This allows you to promote growth, not blame. If you are a people leader, cultivate a growth mindset in others by sharing your failures and the lessons learned.

> *"Your fear of failure and your self-limiting beliefs create imaginary barriers you are convinced you can't break through."*

Where are you stuck? In a job, relationships, financially, health? What limiting beliefs are holding you back, and more importantly, what would you do if they weren't?

We will delve more into how we view and deal with failure in Part Three, but for now, it's time to take back control.

TAKE BACK CONTROL

Are you creating the life you truly deserve, or are you just trying to survive the life you have? Imagine a typical day. You come home after a long day of work, take off your bra (yes guys, that is the first thing we do), take a deep breath, and get ready to start your second shift. No time to process the meeting you just left or the pile of work still on your desk. Now it's time to pick up the mail, drive to soccer practice, pick up dry cleaning, cook dinner, feed the dog, clean the kitchen, pack lunches, fill out field trip paperwork, donate to the umpteenth cause this year, do a load of laundry, and fall into bed exhausted. But don't go to sleep just yet! After two full-time jobs, now it's time to play some Barry White and get your lovin' on. Most nights, I'd rather go for Netflix and ice cream, but hey, gotta keep the love alive!

Something inevitably wakes you in the middle of the night. Last night for me it was the dog hacking and ultimately vomiting under the bed (then I had that moment where I thought, "How bad will it be if I wait until the morning to clean it up? I'm not going to have time to do it then. Should I go back to sleep?" And then I debated with myself whether to clean up the mess or fall back asleep. I chose sleep. I'll never notice the stain under the bed). The alarm screams at 6:00 am, and it's time to do the *whole thing over again.*

If this sounds at all familiar, the question boils down to: Are you living deliberately and purposefully, or do you spend most of your time reacting?

*"Are you living deliberately and purposefully,
or do you spend most of your time reacting?"*

If you've ever looked at your caller ID, only to see a number that makes your stomach drop, you are reacting. If you have ever seen someone walking down the hall and you consciously chose to avoid this person, you are reacting. And if you get caught up in your inbox fighting other people's fires and crises, only to look up and realize its noon before you've gotten anything done on your to-do list, you are reacting. Unfortunately, if you aren't careful, each day becomes the same day. Rather than creating the life you want, you end up with the one you choose to live.

Any time you are reacting, you are subconsciously relinquishing control. When this happens, you lose the ability to think logically or handle a situation calmly. This sidetracks you from your goals and makes you less resilient.

> *"Rather than creating the life you want, you*
> *end up with the one you choose to live."*

For instance, imagine you have been trying to make progress all week on an important project that's been hanging over your head. The phone rings—again! It's that boss (or coworker or client or customer) who just won't leave you alone. You curse under your breath and answer with an abrupt, impatient, "Hello?"

Your chest feels tight, your breathing gets short and shallow, and your heart races. You've been triggered, ambushed by the amygdala that generates a stressed out, fearful response. This primitive part of the brain evolved to keep you safe and helped your ancestors avoid jaguars, bears, poisonous snakes, and other life-threatening dangers. But in the early twenty-first century, you face countless circumstances each day that can set you off in a cascade of emotional reaction, all based on a perceived threat.

Research has documented a connection between how emotionally reactive you are and symptoms of depression, anxiety, and stress.[5] Strong negative emotional reactions such as anger, fear, and frustration can damage your health when they become how you habitually react in stressful situations. They also disrupt your productivity and creativity and can harm your relationships.

Where in your life are you most reactive? Is it at home? Work? With a specific issue or person? This isn't about overhauling everything in your life. Practicing Mind Over Moment is about making subtle choices in the moment to take back control. Practice becoming aware of your thoughts and feelings in the moment so that you can purposefully choose how you respond. This puts you back in the driver's seat and allows you to control your day rather than reacting through it.

"Practice becoming aware of your thoughts and feelings in the moment so that you can purposefully choose how you respond."

BREAK OUT OF REACTIVITY

Do you check your phone the minute you get out of bed? Congratulations! You just gave someone else permission to take control of your brain. Shawn Achor, author of *The Happiness Advantage* and *Big Potential*, notes that the first and last 30 minutes of the day are the times when you are most vulnerable to having your attention hijacked. During these times, your brain is not as easily able to prioritize information or place it into a greater context. By relinquishing control first thing in the morning, you spend the rest of the day trying to recover.

I have to make a conscious effort not to check email first thing in the morning. I remind myself that I've never woken up to an email congratulating me for winning the lottery. There is usually a reminder about something I need to do, somewhere I need to go, or someone I need to call. It is all too easy to let your attention and emotions get hijacked first thing in the morning. It's tempting to want to turn on the news as soon as I wake up. With all of the coronavirus updates and societal unrest, it's easy to be consumed by it. Fear and panic have become normalized and seem to be showing up everywhere. In reality, my email and the news will still be there after I've had time to breathe, drink a cup of coffee, and sit quietly with my dogs. And I will be more equipped to handle it.

Do you find yourself habitually checking social media? Whether it's standing in line at a grocery store or riding an elevator, our need to check status, likes, comments, and be "in the know" is sapping our mental energy. Social media can be great if it helps you connect with others and build relationships, but not when it starts impacting your mood or causes you to constantly compare yourself with others. Doing that is just waging mental war with yourself. The next time you find yourself heading for a social media fix, ask yourself if it is serving you. Is it lifting you up? And is this the right time to distract your attention away from what really matters right now? Will you always make the right choice? Of course not, you are human. That doesn't mean the next choice can't be better.

The only thing you can really control is where you attune your attention. When you are stressed, you are attuned to that. You can numb it by going on Facebook for an hour, but what have you accomplished? Practice being intentional and consciously choose where you want to focus your attention and time.

In order to get out of reaction mode, you must first be aware you are in it. The more time you spend reacting, the more stressed you will feel. Something as simple as turning off push notifications can make a big difference. A simple ding, vibration, or flash of light is enough to distract your attention. It takes time to get back into a state of flow, the state you're in when you are immersed in a task and lose track of time because you're enjoying it.

> *"In order to get out of reaction mode, you must first be aware you are in it."*

You and you alone are responsible for taking back control of your life. Is it easy? Of course not. Will you do it flawlessly? Not unless you are a robot. You are a work in progress. Building resilience requires you pay attention to the choices you are making, the thoughts you are having, and the life you are living. That is Mind Over Moment. The next step toward breaking out of reactivity is to assess your relationship with stress.

YOUR RELATIONSHIP WITH STRESS

For many people, stress is like a bad boss. We try our best to avoid it, but it still pops up at the most inopportune times and manages to make us miserable. Or it's always there behind the glass partition of our mental "office," looking over our shoulders, ready to pounce.

For others, stress is an excuse for emotional release: Things go wrong and they pitch a fit like a toddler having a tantrum. They may feel better for a short time, but then the stress starts building again like a teakettle on the stove. The heat in our lives may be simmering or boiling over, and it's only a matter of time before that high-pitched whistle sends us scrambling yet again.

Stress can feel like an unseen force, like the gravity that drives the tides, always in the background, keeping you on edge, unable to fully relax and expecting the worst rather than looking for the best. Stress can make you feel out of control, disempowered, and at the mercy of forces outside yourself.

Your reactions to stressful situations—including racing heartbeat, shortened breath, muscular tension, and narrowed visual focus—are

"Your reactions to stressful situations are evolutionary adaptations that helped keep your ancestors safe from danger."

evolutionary adaptations that helped keep your ancestors safe from danger. The ones who reacted the fastest when the cobra or tiger struck lived and mated with other survivors, passing along their genes to future generations.

Your body perceives stress as a series of physiological responses to external pressures and problems arise when you are under prolonged or chronic stress.[6] Chronic stress has been linked to increased risk of anxiety, depression, digestive problems, headaches, heart disease, sleep problems, weight gain, and impaired memory and concentration, just to name a few.

According to the Mayo Clinic, "The long-term activation of the stress-response system, and the overexposure to cortisol and other stress hormones that follows, can disrupt almost all your body's processes."[7]

Even if you thrive on stress, that doesn't mean it's a good thing. Stress addicts may pride themselves on their frenetic lives, but they are no more invincible than people who are addicted to substances like meth or crack. And like other addicts, sooner or later they will crash—whether it's through occupational burnout, anxiety and depression, physical health problems, or all of the above.

People kept telling me to take care of myself. I was under tremendous stress, trying to balance raising two kids—one of whom has some pretty intense special needs—with running my business and wearing my many other hats as a wife, daughter, volunteer, friend, etc. When people asked if I was sleeping, my response was a sarcastic: "I'll sleep when I'm dead." When friends told me to relax, I thought, "Ok, I'll just take time off and have a spa day" (insert sarcasm here). I didn't have time to relax.

"When you don't take time to manage your stress, life has a way of stopping you in your tracks."

Unfortunately, when you don't take time to manage your stress, life has a way of stopping you in your tracks. My body was worn down, my immune system exhausted, and it ultimately resulted in a tumor in my salivary gland. In my book *Strong Enough,* I recounted the ridiculous series of events that followed my diagnosis. Left unchecked and unaddressed, stress will take a toll. I'll never forget what I said when my doctor told me that I had a tumor in my face. My actual response was, "I don't have time for a tumor." Apparently, tumors don't take your timetable into account.

According to one study, in a survey of nearly one thousand women, 56 percent of women said work stress has negatively impacted their personal relationships.[8] Seventy-two percent said they feel either drained, exhausted, or anxious at the end of the day, and 42 percent said they felt inferior after visiting Pinterest (who the hell can make cupcakes look that good?). Another study shows women who work 41 to 50 hours a week have elevated risks for conditions such as heart disease, arthritis, and diabetes—all much higher numbers than the risks found in men who work the same amount.[9]

BEAT BURNOUT

You are bombarded by information, saturated with digital stimulation, and there always seems to be more to do than time to do it. It is no surprise that the World Health Organization recently recognized "burnout" as a syndrome resulting from chronic workplace stress.[10] I would argue that for many of us, it isn't just the workplace but the combination of stressors in our careers, families, and lives in general that lead to burnout.

Symptoms of burnout include feelings of energy depletion or exhaustion, increased mental distance from your job, feelings of negativity or cynicism related to work, and reduced productivity. Sound familiar?

My daughter Rylee just graduated high school, and the amount of stress these kids are under is mind boggling. Teenagers are riddled with anxiety over grades, fitting in, getting into college, being perceived as smart, and so much more. Throw in hormones, unfamiliar emotions, peer pressure, and a global pandemic to boot, and you have a perfect storm. By the time teenagers enter adulthood, many are already feeling worn down.

So how can you manage the stress that's causing you to feel burned out? Mind Over Moment allows you to create a purposeful plan to start addressing it, rather than reacting to it. Yet many people find themselves where I was a few years ago—feeling so exhausted, so overwhelmed, and so discouraged that they find it hard to even start addressing what is making them feel that way.

When I was dealing with feelings of burnout, I turned to the same lessons that I teach others to help me cope. The most important principle is to start by making small changes because subtle changes repeated over time bring big results. So even though my stressors did not change, I started proactively doing things to manage my response:

- I took up swimming.
- I started a gratitude journal.
- I learned how to meditate.
- I got curious about my emotions and went to therapy.

If I had tried to tackle all of these at once I would have felt overwhelmed and not done any of them. So, I took them one at a time. And gradually those feelings of being burned out, exhausted, and stuck began to lift. Does that mean I never feel burned out? Of course not, but practicing these habits has helped minimize the amount of time I spend there.

Trying to juggle all the things you have going on can be exhausting. It can also be an opportunity to build resilience. Which beliefs, habits, and behaviors are helping you manage the stress in your life? Which ones could be undermining your success?

CHANGE YOUR VIEW OF STRESS

A growing body of research has shown that your belief about stress and the way you cope is often more important than the stress itself.[11] Now, the idea that you can take a healthier view of stress does not deny the fact that chronic stress, left unaddressed, is associated with serious health problems, from high blood pressure and heart disease to anxiety and depression, but how you think about stress matters.

"Your belief about stress and the way you cope is often more important than the stress itself."

In her book, *The Upside of Stress*, Stanford psychologist and lecturer Kelly McGonigal says that learning to view stress more positively helps people cope in ways that allow them to thrive.[12] She cites research by Stanford psychology Assistant Professor Alia Crum showing that viewing stress as a helpful part of life, rather than as harmful, is associated with better health, emotional well-being, and productivity at work—even during periods of high stress.

The way you cope is often determined by the way you perceive the stress itself. I've had many a day where I felt overwhelmed and stressed, and the only thing I wanted was a cheeseburger, fries, a shake, and a good episode of *Law and Order SVU*. When I'm in that place, I'm more likely to get stuck in "what ifs" and worst-case scenarios. I procrastinate dealing with the issue at hand because everything feels daunting. Now don't get me wrong. There are absolutely times when I go that route and let my mind run away, but I am aware that it is a choice that I am making. I give myself grace and make a different choice next time.

Conversely, there are other times when I view stress as my body preparing itself, putting on armor, getting ready for action. In those times, I'm more likely to exercise, eat foods that give me fuel, and get plenty of rest. I go into problem solving mode, take time to think, and make a plan of action.

How you think about stress matters. Your body believes the messages you send yourself and your stress response will match accordingly. McGonigal sites a study that tracked 30,000 individuals over eight years.[13] The researchers started by asking two questions: (1) What level of stress have you had in the past 12 months (low, moderate, high)? and (2) Do you think stress is bad for you? People who experienced high levels of stress the year before had a 43 percent increased risk of dying prematurely, but it was only true for the people who believed stress was harmful to their health. The people who had high levels of stress but did not believe stress was bad for them had the lowest risk of dying of anyone in the study, even less than those who had minimal stress!

"How you think about stress matters."

As McGonigal explains, "Instead of viewing sweating and increased heartbeat as a threat, what if you viewed it as energizing, preparing you to meet the challenge? Your pounding heart—preparing you for action. Breathing faster—more oxygen to your brain. Blood surging—you are dilating your blood vessels to increase blood flow and boost performance."[14]

Stress also makes you seek social connection. When you are under stress, your body produces stress hormones such as adrenaline and cortisol that trigger the fight-or-flight reflex, but it also produces another neurohormone: oxytocin.

You've probably heard of this hormone because of its cute nick-names, "the cuddle hormone" and the "tend and befriend" hormone. As McGonigal notes in her 2015 TED Talk *Making Stress Your Friend*, "when oxytocin is released as a stress response, it is motivating you to seek support. It fine-tunes your brain's social instincts and primes you to do things that strengthen close relationships. Oxytocin makes you crave physical contact with your friends and family and even enhances your empathy. It makes you more willing to help and support the people you care about."[15]

Transform Your Stress Response

Can you really alleviate the harmful effects of stress by changing your response to it? The short answer, based on numerous scientific studies, is yes. Because responses to stress are triggered in the brain, you can protect yourself from the most damaging effects of stress by changing how you interpret and respond to difficult circumstances.

When you are under stress, the amygdala, the emotional processing center of the brain, lights up, activating the fight-or-flight response. You face countless circumstances each day that can trigger a cascade of emotional reaction, all based on a perceived threat. Overstimulation of the amygdala has been linked to anxiety and can harm your physical health. It disrupts your productivity and creativity and often harms relationships.

"You can protect yourself from the most damaging effects of stress by changing how you interpret and respond to difficult circumstances."

Anytime your fight-or-flight response is activated, you have been emotionally hijacked. Imagine you are in a meeting. You go into the meeting already feeling overwhelmed and are considering asking for help or relief from your boss and co-workers. Then unexpectedly, your boss assigns you an additional project with a short deadline. Immediately, your heart races, your palms sweat, and your stomach tightens. You have just been emotionally hijacked.

When you have been emotionally hijacked, you no longer have access to the prefrontal cortex, the part of the brain responsible for higher level thinking, problem solving, creativity, decision making, abstract thinking, and emotional regulation. Yet that is exactly the part of the brain you need to access in order to short-circuit the stress response. This can be difficult to do in the heat of the moment, and it takes practice. We will explore the process in a bit.

You can take steps to reduce the external pressures you are under, but because that's not always possible, changing your response to stress is the single most important thing you can do to protect your health and sanity.

Research shows that stress is destructive, until the moment you believe it isn't.[16] Changing the way you think about stress changes the effect stress has on your body. McGonigal's research has found that the best way to manage stress isn't to reduce or avoid it, but rather to rethink it, even embrace it. If you believe stress is harmful, you are more likely to cope in unhelpful, even harmful, ways to help numb or escape the discomfort.

> *"Changing the way you think about stress*
> *changes the effect stress has on your body."*

The next time you find yourself feeling stressed, be mindful of how your body responds (such as shallow breathing and increased heart rate) and try to see these responses as helpful rather than debilitating. Recognize that stress is something everyone deals with. Not only can you handle it, you can grow from it as well.

This has been difficult to practice with Evan. His brain is in an almost constant state of fight or flight. The part of his brain that regulates emotions doesn't function correctly and causes him to perceive things as a threat, whether they are or not. It has been profound for me to learn to regulate, because you can't help someone else regulate their behavior if you can't regulate your own. While Evan continues to learn skills and coping mechanisms, his brain is constantly in battle. We have practiced deep breathing, yoga, and meditation. While he has made significant improvements, that doesn't mean we stop practicing. It might take a little longer, but he is learning, and so are we.

What is one thing you can do today to start inching your way toward changes that will make you more resilient to stress? Start by examining how you respond when you feel overwhelmed. Do you become tense, distracted, irritable, or short with the people around you? Do you have trouble sleeping and constantly feel tired? Your body is talking to you. Listen to it. Start proactively recognizing the signs before stress causes you to freeze up. Simply recognizing the pattern is enough to interrupt it.

Resilience is not about the amount of stress or trauma you face, but the way you process it, view it, and manage it. When you stop running away from stress and start to view it as a normal part of facing life's challenges, you can pursue what gives your life meaning and trust yourself to handle the stress that follows.

RETHINK "BUSY"

When people ask how you're doing, what do you say? My 94-year-old, 4'9" grandmother says, "Honey, I'm fantastic. If I were any better, I'd be twins. At this point, heaven is a lateral move." Most people aren't quite as enthusiastic when asked how they are doing (although behind me on a plane once was a guy who, when asked by the flight attendant how he was doing, responded, "I'm kickin' like a chicken").

"Busy does not equal productive.
Busy equals exhausted."

If you pay attention, when we ask others how they are doing, they often reply with "busy," "crazy busy," or "stressed and busy." How often do you tell yourself or others how busy you are? In our culture, we wear "busyness" as a badge of honor. Pretty soon the Girl Scouts are going to start passing out "busy badges." We believe being busy means we are getting a lot done. But busy does not equal productive. Busy equals exhausted.

Busy has become a way of life. It's almost an absolute. The sky is up, the ground is down, rain is wet, and I am busy. Being busy often means racing to put out one fire after the next and getting to the end of the day realizing you haven't done anything to make headway on what is most important to you.

Being busy wears down your resilience, like your car running on fumes when you run the tank down too low. You hit a bump in the road and next thing you know, you're out of gas.

When you tell yourself how busy you are (even if it's true), you put yourself in a reactive rather than a strategic, proactive stance. You put aside the things that aren't screaming for your attention (even things that could help you work smarter, be more productive, and feel happier) and focus on putting out fires. You put your head down, your nose to the grindstone, and you multitask.

When you find yourself reacting, simply taking a moment to acknowledge it is enough to help you take back control. Notice your racing thoughts, quickened pulse, and tightened muscles. The goal of Mind Over Moment is to recognize these feelings and sensations, observe them, and then decide if they are serving you.

BE WHERE YOU ARE WHEN YOU'RE THERE

We have a finite amount of attention, so it is important to be deliberate about where we focus it. Unfortunately, we tend to do the opposite. A 2010 study by Harvard psychologists Matthew A. Killingsworth and Daniel T. Gilbert found we spend 47 percent of our time thinking about something other than what we are doing in the moment.[17] I can only imagine that since 2010, this number has grown dramatically.

"We have a finite amount of attention,
so it is important to be deliberate about
where we focus it."

Have you ever had the experience of going over the exact same things in two meetings because nothing got accomplished in the first meeting? It was probably because everybody was somewhere else mentally.

Jay and the kids laugh at me because we will watch a movie that we've already seen, and I honestly don't remember seeing it the first time! I swore up and down I had never seen *The Avengers*. I probably could have passed a lie detector test. When Jay produced a movie stub as proof along with an "I told you so," I was blown away. While I was in the theater, I must have been thinking about a million different things. Some new business idea, the kids' homework, a new keynote, what we were going to have for dinner, why zebras have stripes, or any number of other random stuff that goes through my mind. I may have been there physically, but I certainly wasn't present.

How many times do you catch yourself not being present? When you do, you are practicing Mind Over Moment. You are catching yourself behaving out of habit and making a conscious effort to behave differently. When you are truly present, you are both productive and engaged—focused on accomplishing the tasks before you and building and strengthening relationships.

Recently I was on a plane getting ready to take off when the woman sitting next to me got a call. She answered and started FaceTiming with her two kids—loudly. Everybody within 10 rows could hear her conversation, some of them started looking annoyed, and I caught myself feeling the same way. But then, as I listened to her conversation (because it was impossible not to) I realized she was completely focused on her kids. She said, "So tell me about your teacher." And one of her kids replied: "She's great, I really like her," to which the mom responded, "Tell me why."

People were getting annoyed with her because she was so loud, but I started thinking about how awesome it was that she cared about her kids' day so much. She wasn't just saying "uh-huh" like parents often do;

she was genuinely curious. I realized I want to have more conversations like that with my kids. Maybe just not that loudly while on an airplane.

So how can you be less "busy" and distracted and more present and focused? This is where Mind Over Moment comes in. Mind Over Moment means taking the time to pause and be deliberate about all the choices you make, large and small. If you think you don't have time, think again. Because the truth is, you can decide how you want to live through every moment of your life. You make time for what's most important to you. Period.

Stop Multitasking

Multitasking isn't just doing multiple things at once. It includes all kinds of distractions when you are doing one thing but thinking about something else. According to Harvard Medical School, "Multitasking has become a way of life."[18] The average office worker switches what they are doing every three minutes and five seconds.[19] People talk on a cell phone while commuting to work or scan the news while returning emails. But in the rush to accomplish necessary tasks, people often lose connection with the present moment. They stop being truly attentive to what they are doing or feeling.

Trying to do multiple things at once and constantly switching tasks is bad for your stress levels, mental health, and productivity.[20] The results can be disastrous, comical, or both.

While working with a business client, I asked their team for examples of multitasking gone awry. One executive told me how he was on the phone with his wife while texting his assistant. He accidentally sent his assistant the message: "XO XO can't wait to see you tonight, give you a big squeeze." Oops.

Most of us are more prone to multitask when we are under stress. The more we do this, the harder it is to stop. Interestingly, the more we multitask, the more we lower our attention threshold. Prolonged exposure to the stress hormone cortisol can actually shrink the brain and the gray matter that allows us to focus our attention, control our emotions, and think clearly.[21] This makes it harder to break habits such as multitasking. See the irony?

A University of London study found that multimedia tasking, like watching TV and playing a game at the same time, causes a greater decline in IQ points than smoking marijuana or going 24 hours without sleep. [22]

Women often pride themselves on multitasking, but we are the worst offenders. On average, men do one-and-a-half things at once while women, especially mothers, do closer to five things at once. One study found that moms multitask about 10 hours a week more than dads.[23] Unfortunately, it doesn't make us more productive, but it does increase negative emotions, stress, anxiety, depression, and perceived work/life balance conflict.

Mind Over Moment is the opposite of multitasking. It means you focus attention on what is happening in the present and accept it without judgment. Learn to catch yourself when you are multitasking and reset what you are doing to focus on completing one task at a time.

TAKE CONTROL OF DIGITAL DISTRACTIONS

Many of us, me included, are addicted to our smartphones. According to the latest statistics, we check our devices an average of 80 times a day (that is every 12 minutes.) The average time we spend on our phones each day is fast approaching three hours. When time on other devices is factored in, it's more than four-and-a-half hours a day. We tap, swipe, or click on our phones an average of 2,617 times each day.[24]

Ironically, all the time we spend on devices seeking to stay connected is making us feel less connected with ourselves and others. When 85 percent of us check our devices while speaking with friends and family, we cannot be fully present for others. We give a five-inch piece of hardware with no pulse more time and attention than the people in our lives.

Our digital addiction is blamed for increased anxiety, stress, depression, loneliness, self-absorption, sleep deprivation, and attention deficit disorder. One study found increasing smartphone usage temporarily diminishes the ability to interpret the deeper meaning of information.[25]

Dr. David Greenfield, founder and medical director of the Center for Internet and Technology Addiction, says, "We're carrying our drug with us—our digital drug—everywhere we go." He explains, "the internet is the world's largest slot machine, it's not a logical thing. It bypasses the frontal lobes of the brain."[26]

Do you use your phone purposefully or habitually? On an elevator? God forbid you talk to someone. You should check your phone. In the line at the grocery store? Don't stand quietly, giving your mind time to rest—check your Facebook page instead. In a bathroom stall? Ladies, you know what to do. We give this little piece of hardware so much time, attention, and energy. Once I was in a women's room at the airport while someone was talking on their speaker phone! There are some things you just don't need to hear!

Simply having your phone on the table at lunch or in meetings makes you appear less engaged. Greenfield explains that, "seeing your phone makes you more likely to pick it up to see what's happening elsewhere while missing what's right in front of you." We are so worried about missing out, that we end up missing out.

For many of us, having our phone is a security blanket, keeping us from being bored or lonely. Guess what? It's okay to be bored. Our need to fill every single second with entertainment means that we don't have the time to just be still, giving our minds a rest from working so hard and constantly being on alert. And we are teaching our kids to do the same.

"Having our phone is a security blanket, keeping us from being bored or lonely. Guess what? It's okay to be bored."

I started tracking my phone usage each week, and I've got to tell you, if I spent nearly as much time exercising as I do on my phone, I'd be able to fit into everything in my closet. The next time you are waiting for a flight or meeting, take a moment to observe everyone around you. I've started doing this and have been blown away by the number of people on their devices.

Last month I treated myself to a massage. While in the tranquil, serene waiting room with a running fountain and soft music, every single person was glued to their device. If you are taking a moment to relax and recharge, disconnect from the thing that is part of the reason you need to relax and recharge.

Stay mindful of when and why you are using your phone and devices. If the goal is to numb anxiety, minimize boredom, and check out, try closing your eyes and taking a few deep breaths. Stillness can be profound. Most of us just don't take time to experience it.

RESILIENCE REQUIRES COURAGE

A resilient mindset requires courage and grit because it forces you to challenge comfortable patterns. I used to think that courage and fear were at opposite ends of the spectrum. I questioned how I could possibly be brave while being terrified. I now know that true courage means being afraid or uncomfortable and doing what you need to do anyway. Some days courage means you just show up. It means you roll out of bed exhausted, manage to find matching shoes, drive to work while shaving or applying makeup, drop your kids off while they're screaming, spill coffee on your brand-new shirt—but you show up.

There were so many days with Evan that coming home required courage. Yes, I was afraid of the rage and aggression, but I was more afraid I would lose my temper and lash out at Evan and the rest of my family. Courage meant sitting in the driveway to take a few deep breaths before entering the house. Courage meant forgiving myself when I fell short.

Courage can be having a difficult conversation, speaking up, or having clear boundaries. Perhaps my favorite definition of courage comes from Mary Ann Radmacher, who says, "Courage doesn't always roar. Sometimes courage is the quiet voice at the end of the day saying, I'll try again tomorrow." I talk more about courage in my book *Strong Enough*.

We run from discomfort, but it is where resilience is built. Discomfort is a catalyst for growth. Successful people have fear, self-doubt, and insecurity, so if you feel those things, you're in good company.

Just remember this: If you're not afraid or uncomfortable, it's probably not courage. Carefully hear with your heart and soul what I am about to say, because this is the truth: Whatever happens, at the end of the day, *you will either succeed or you will survive.*

> "Whatever happens, at the end of the day,
> you will either succeed or you will survive."

RESILIENCE TAKES GRIT

In her book *Grit*, Angela Duckworth defines grit as a combination of passion and perseverance toward long-term goals.[27] Grit is the willingness to lean in when it would be easier to let go.

A lot of people think that grit and resilience are synonymous, but they're not. Grit is rugged determination, passion, and perseverance toward a goal that is important to you. It's how you approach something that you're doggedly determined to accomplish. In pursuit of that goal, or in life in general, you're going to get knocked down. Resilience is your ability to not only get back up, but to get back up stronger. It's your ability to not just survive challenging times and overcome adversity but to grow and thrive because of it.

To build grit, Duckworth suggests:

- Use the word "yet." Instead of saying you can't do something or don't know how, say you can't do it or don't know how to do it *yet*. Can I change a tire? I'm embarrassed to say I cannot. At least not *yet*.

- If you're struggling with willpower or making the right choices, create an if/then agreement. If there are donuts, then I will eat fruit. If I am bored, then I will go for a 10-minute walk. The more specific, the better.

Some have argued that there are times when it is possible to have too much grit. There is something to be said for realizing when stretching for a goal is undermining your real priorities, or when pursuit of that goal is no longer healthy. Although that may be true, only you know if your goals are worth chasing.

Here's the question I ask myself when I start to feel discouraged: "Am I thinking about giving up because the goal isn't worth it or because I'm afraid?" Nine times out of 10, the answer is fear.

MAXIMIZE YOUR MINDSET

Your mindset, beliefs, and habits are your toolbox for building resilience. Without this foundation, skills will only take you so far. The good news is that these are all things under your control and developing them is a life-long process. Mind Over Moment is a practice, meaning there is no perfect, but rather a constant pursuit for improvement.

There will be days where you kick ass and other days where your ass will be kicked. That's all part of the journey.

—— Part Two: ——
SKILLSET

If you think of your mindset as your toolbox, your skills are the tools that fill it. This skillset includes how you manage emotions and stress, mitigate negative self-talk, and engage in activities that build resilience, like humor, social connection, mindfulness, and self-care. These tools help you manage stress, navigate change and uncertainty, and bounce back more easily from setbacks.

At the heart of Mind Over Moment and your ability to build resilience is the skill of emotional intelligence.

RESILIENCE AND EMOTIONAL INTELLIGENCE

Emotional intelligence (EI) or emotional quotient (EQ) is the ability to recognize and understand emotions in yourself and others, and to use this awareness to manage your behavior and relationships. Your resilience is directly related to your emotional intelligence. Your brain stem takes all your senses and puts them in your brain for processing. Information goes first through the reptilian brain (your primitive brain), then to the limbic system (the emotional center of the brain), and finally moves to the prefrontal cortex (the logical thinking part of the brain). You have emotional reactions to everything that happens in your life, whether you are aware of them or not. The more intense your emotions, the more likely they are to dictate your actions and behavior. Your emotional brain works 80,000 times faster than your logical brain, meaning that it is neurologically impossible to have a logical thought without emotion driving it.[28]

Your emotional intelligence determines how you make decisions, relate to others, view yourself, and so much more. People with a higher EQ are better able to form lasting, positive relationships, adapt to changing conditions in their environment, and be a positive influence on others.

"It is neurologically impossible to have a logical thought without emotion driving it."

Research by Travis Bradberry and Jean Greaves in their book *Emotional Intelligence 2.0* shows that emotional intelligence is the strongest predictor of performance in the workplace and the strongest driver of leadership and personal success.[29] EQ accounts for 58 percent of success in all kinds of jobs. Among top business performers, 90 percent score high in EQ, and 80 percent of bottom performers score low in EQ. It is the biggest differentiator between average and star performers, and the link between EQ and earnings is so direct that every point increase in EQ adds $1,300 to an annual salary.[30]

What fascinates me is that there is no connection between your EQ and IQ. In fact, 70 percent of the time, someone with an average IQ will outperform someone with an exceptionally high IQ. Have you ever met someone who is brilliant but has no social skills? If not, it could be you. Just sayin'.

In short, EQ is your ability to recognize your own mood through self-awareness, intentionally change it through self-management, understand its impact on others through social awareness, and behave in a way that lifts the mood of others through relationship management.

GROW YOUR EMOTIONAL INTELLIGENCE

Everyone has strengths and opportunities to grow when it comes to emotional intelligence. You may be very self-aware but struggle with empathy. Or you may be able to empathize with others but have difficulty regulating your emotions.

The good news is that you are not born with a set level of emotional intelligence. EQ is nothing more than a collection of skills and habits. Like all skills worth acquiring, building emotional intelligence takes practice.

Emotional intelligence begins with self-awareness. Be aware of the mood you bring into the room when you show up. Is the room better when you enter it or when you leave it? Would your colleagues and friends agree? How does your mood show up at work, and how does it affect the people around you? What percentage of your day are you happy, sad, excited, frustrated, or mad?

> *"How does your mood show up at work, and how does it affect the people around you?"*

Make conscious decisions about how you go through your day. Remember, the more you think and behave a certain way, the easier it is to think and behave that way. In a grumpy mood? If you stay there long enough, that can become your default way of thinking. The same is true for anxiety, fear, and worry. On the upside, the more time you spend grateful, present, calm, and kind, the easier it is to stay there as well.

A coach I worked with a few years ago said something that will stick with me forever. I often started my sentences with, "I'm struggling with…" I was struggling with Evan, work, stress, love, and so many other things. One day she stopped me and said, "Do you realize that you are addicted to struggle." Whoa. I'm not often speechless, but that did it. The more I thought about it, the more I realized how right she was. I was addicted to struggle, stress, and frustration. It might not have been nicotine or alcohol, but I was an addict. I started to pay attention to how my mood and emotions impacted me and everyone around me.

How are you showing up? Think about emotions that detract from your effectiveness (annoyed, angry, gloomy, anxious, fearful, nervous) as opposed to emotions that enhance your effectiveness (joyful, playful, inspired, adventurous, grateful, amazed, imaginative, cheerful).

Everyone has blind spots. A blind spot is an area of your personality or behavior that other people see, that you may not. You might think you are hilarious, yet someone else might perceive you as obnoxious. You may see yourself as shy, yet others might view you as distant.

To learn how you show up, ask for feedback regularly. Feedback and reactions from others are a key ingredient to building emotional intelligence. The challenge is that when you get feedback, it's easy to fall into the trap of justifying and defending your behavior.

I observed a feedback conversation with one of my clients and her employee. It went like this:

Employee: Can you please give me some constructive feedback to help me improve?

Manager: One opportunity is to allow others to finish what they are saying without interrupting.

Employee: Yes, but it's just because I don't want to forget what I'm going to say. Can you give me some more feedback?

Manager: Well, sometimes you raise your voice, and it can be off-putting.

Employee: It's just because I feel really passionate about this, and I want you to know how much it matters to me. Can you give me some more feedback?

You get the idea. No one wants to give feedback to someone who justifies and defends his/her behavior. Instead, if someone is willing to give you feedback, take it as a gift. You don't have to agree with it, but it's worth taking a closer look.

A great way to ask for specific feedback is to ask for advice. Instead of, "Can you give me some feedback about how I handle conflict," you might try, "If you could give me one piece of advice to help me better manage conflict, what would it be?"

Then, listen without justifying or defending. If you feel yourself starting to escalate, try asking a question (and not a question like, "What is your problem?"). Instead try, "That's interesting, could you give me a specific example?" Or "I hadn't thought about it that way. Can you tell me more?"

The next time you receive feedback, try this statement, "Thank you for the feedback. I'd like to take some time to digest it." Feedback is a gift, and if someone is being vulnerable enough to share it, take it in the spirit with which it's given and process it and your emotions before responding.

Rather than shutting people down because you get defensive, this allows the other person to be heard. It may also give you some valuable advice and input. Just because you receive feedback doesn't mean you have to agree with it or act on it, but it does help you build self-awareness.

My Grammy used to say, "Annie, if enough people tell you you're tired, maybe it's time to lay down." If enough people give you similar feedback, there is probably some truth to it.

She also used to say, "If you act like an ass, don't be surprised if people try to ride you," but that's another conversation all together.

Remember the growth mindset? Someone with a fixed mindset is more likely to get defensive, argumentative, or passive aggressive after receiving feedback. When you have a growth mindset, you reflect on feedback, identifying areas where you can improve.

EMOTIONAL REGULATION

Your emotional health and well-being are tied directly to your ability to regulate your emotions.

Evan started early childhood intervention therapy when he was just 11 months old and has been in some form of therapy ever since. Although therapists have different approaches, all of them told us that we can't help Evan regulate his emotions when we are dysregulated.

When you are in a conversation that escalates into conflict, it's like watching a tennis match. One person gets louder and faster, the other person matches, and it goes back and forth until someone inevitably yells, "YOU NEED TO CALM DOWN!"

Now, I don't know if you've ever said that to someone or if someone has said it to you, but in my experience, there is no better way to frustrate me than to tell me to calm down. "I AM CALM!" is typically my response. You cannot help someone regulate their emotions when you can't regulate your own.

Raising Evan has been an eye-opening emotional intelligence building exercise. It has put a magnifier on my own behavior. It's almost like being outside of myself, watching someone else handle explosive situations poorly. I have shed countless tears beating myself up over losing my cool or saying the wrong thing.

I'll never forget the time I gave a speech to 4,000 teachers about emotional intelligence. I spent the last 20 minutes of the speech teaching them how to help regulate their emotions and the emotions of their students. I was brilliant if I do say so myself. But then I got home to find

Rylee crying, Evan screaming, Jay angry, and the dogs going nuts, and I lost my damn mind. I yelled, I cried, I apologized, and I forgave myself. We are all a work in progress.

The great news is that you can interrupt the cycle to take back control by identifying your triggers.

Get to Know Your Triggers

A trigger is an internal or external stimulus that causes you to have a knee-jerk reaction that may not be the best reaction to a situation. Once you have been triggered, your emotional brain goes into protection mode. You lose the ability to access your prefrontal cortex, which means that logic flies out the window. The first step toward managing your emotions is to identify your triggers.

Everyone has triggers that stimulate emotions such as anger, jealousy, embarrassment, and guilt. My mom used to get triggered when I rolled my eyes. I thought it was the dumbest thing to be triggered by until I had my own daughter. Apparently, eye rolling is a trigger that has been passed down through generations.

Start to identify triggers by paying close attention to your physical and psychological responses. For example, I often get triggered when I'm embarrassed. My shoulders tighten, my hands get clammy, my heart races, and I become self-critical. I know that when those things are happening, I have been triggered.

Does your chest feel tight? Is your breathing shallow? Are you feeling anxious, rushed, and overwhelmed? By training yourself to periodically stop and check-in with your feelings and physical sensations, you build self-awareness. That makes it easier to catch yourself and reset your response.

Everyone is triggered by different types of threats. For some, it is a challenge to their status or ego; for others, it's being left out of a group conversation or discussion. Mind Over Moment allows you to become aware of your emotional triggers so that you can respond rather than react.

"Mind Over Moment allows you to become aware of your emotional triggers so that you can respond rather than react."

As we navigate COVID-19, the entire world is in a state of uncertainty. Yesterday, more than 1,800 people died from the virus in the United States, and that number is climbing. One of the biggest triggers can be uncertainty. Our brains don't like uncertainty, and there is no shortage of it right now. A University of London study found that volunteers who knew they would get a shock felt calmer and less agitated than those who were told they only had a 50 percent likelihood of being shocked.[31] In times of uncertainty, our brains can't just pause our stress response. It stays on constant alert, waiting to protect us at any moment. Our brains would rather have an outcome that they don't like than one they don't know.

The feeling of anxiety is prevalent right now, and most of it is stemming from uncertainty. You are much more likely to be triggered when your emotional immune system has been worn down.

You can proactively manage triggers by taking the time to think about what causes those knee-jerk reactions or puts you on the defensive before you have a conversation with your kids, your partner, or your boss. Then you can reframe how you want to respond to avoid getting emotionally hijacked.

MANAGE YOUR EMOTIONAL RESPONSES

Once you are aware of your triggers, you can begin to proactively manage your responses. If you touch a hot stove, you don't stand there with your finger on it, contemplating whether or not you should move. You immediately recoil. That is an automatic reaction. Your emotions work much the same way. An emotion is a reaction and a neurobiological response. How you respond is a choice. Your success, in large part, is determined by how you choose to behave, and not how you automatically react.

You may have heard of the saying "name it to tame it." Labeling and naming emotions makes them easier to deal with by taking some of their power away. By putting your feelings into words, you give yourself more control over them. You cannot control what you cannot understand. Although it sounds simple in theory, understanding your emotions is more difficult than you might imagine. A study was conducted with 500,000 people to explore the role of emotions in our daily lives, asking them to name the emotion they were feeling in the moment. Astonishingly, only 36 percent were able to accurately identify their emotions as they were happening.[32]

Rather than judging how you feel, or telling yourself you shouldn't feel that way, try to get curious about your emotions. Is that really anger you're feeling, or are you hurt? If so, why? Are you embarrassed? What about the situation caused you to feel that way? We typically try to push uncomfortable emotions away, and that only serves to increase their intensity and duration, while undermining our ability to deal with them.

Emotions are reactions, but the way you interpret them is a choice. For example, if you feel overwhelmed, what is the story you are telling yourself? "I'm so busy. I have so much to do. I don't know how I will get it all done." The emotion (the feeling of being overwhelmed) is just there to give you information. Assigning judgment and self-doubt is a choice. You can stop to observe the butterflies in your stomach or the tension in your shoulders. Get curious and observe the emotion rather than getting overtaken by it. The truth is that it will all get done and things will work out. You can view this as your body simply gearing up, gaining energy to conquer what's in front of you. You can waste emotional energy worrying about something that may go wrong, or you can take a deep breath and invest your energy to ensure it goes right.

The stories we tell ourselves drive our response, and our response drives the outcome. If you believe that your co-worker Carol woke up with the intent to annoy you, your response will most likely be defensive, closed off, and irritated. Conversely, if you believe that Carol must be having a really tough time, you are more likely to get curious and ask if she is okay. Remember, our beliefs drive our behavior. We can completely alter the outcome, simply by shifting the story we are telling ourselves.

Trust me, this is easier said than done, and there will be times when you fail miserably.

"We can completely alter the outcome, simply by shifting the stories we tell ourselves."

A couple of years ago on Mother's Day, Jay and the kids were kind enough to bring me breakfast in bed. I ate this delicious meal, had a wonderful morning, and then left to run a few errands. As I was heading home, I thought to myself, "I really hope Jay and the kids did the dishes. If they really care about me, they won't make me do the dishes on Mother's Day." Now, I realize this isn't rational, but it's the story I told myself. I visualized the scene in the movie *The Breakup* with Vince Vaughn and Jennifer Aniston. She is standing at the sink, fuming because he didn't do the dishes. Exasperated, she explained that she wanted him to *want* to do the dishes, to which he responded, "You don't want to do the dishes! Why would I want to do the dishes?" I got home, and sure enough, the kitchen was a mess. Everything from breakfast was there, along with the dishes that had piled up throughout the day. Here's what may or may not have gone down:

Trigger: A messy kitchen

Emotion: Disappointment

Thought: If they really wanted to make Mother's Day special, someone would have cleaned the kitchen.

Response: Become passive aggressive. This is where Jay said, "Honey, are you okay?" I responded with an abrupt, "I'm fine," to which he said, "Um, you should probably tell your face."

Outcome: Jay and kids didn't feel appreciated for making breakfast and had no idea why I was distant.

Now, logically, I know that not doing the dishes doesn't equate to not loving me. Looking back it was a missed opportunity to appreciate their kindness. It's also a perfect example of how easy it is for our expectations to become resentments.

If I could go back, I would have practiced Mind Over Moment, observing my natural reaction, and choosing a more appropriate response, explaining to my family how I felt.

In this situation, the messy kitchen was the trigger. I felt disappointed. "If they loved and appreciated me, someone would have done the dishes" may have been my first interpretation of the event, but it doesn't have to be the one I stick with. Maybe they haven't done the dishes *yet*. Or maybe they didn't know it was that important to me or the way I want to be shown love. Thinking about it differently creates a different response and ultimately a different outcome.

We create so much of our own misery simply by the stories we tell ourselves. This is in no way easy, but with Mind Over Moment, you have an opportunity to catch that emotional runaway train before you completely derail.

Thoughts and behaviors become habits. The more you think or act a certain way, the more that thought and behavior becomes ingrained in your brain circuitry. People who learn to choose their interpretation of events in times of stress are more psychologically resilient.

The next time you find yourself triggered, try working through the emotional management process.

- What is the trigger?
- What emotion does it cause?

- What is your thought, interpretation, or story?
- What is your response?
- What is the likely outcome?

Now, think about how you can tweak your interpretation. Chances are that a simple shift in perspective can change the outcome. It also leaves you feeling more in control and less frustrated. Even if you can't seem to change the story you tell yourself, at least you can be aware that you are telling it. Then you can decide how to proceed.

EMBRACE CRAPPY EMOTIONS

Our whole lives, we are taught to run the other way from uncomfortable emotions. "You're sad? Don't be. You have so much to be happy about." "You're heartbroken? You'll get over it. Time heals all wounds."

When was the last time you got swept away by negative emotions? Did you try to push the feelings aside, telling yourself it wasn't that big of a deal? Or did you give yourself time to sit in that discomfort?

When we face grief, loss, or other messy emotions, it's easy to want to run from the discomfort. Although some of our emotions may not feel good, they are all necessary. Sometimes we are so busy judging how we should feel that we forget to just feel.

"Although some of our emotions may not feel good, they are all necessary."

Negative emotions are uncomfortable. We want to hide from them, thinking we will deal with them later. Only there is never a good time. Allowing ourselves the time and space to process emotions is not a luxury, it is a requirement for resilience.

For example, the feeling of anxiety during this pandemic is overwhelming and palpable. It is easy to want to rush past difficult emotions or numb them altogether. So, what can you do? You sit in it, name the emotion, and intentionally choose how you respond. Fear and anxiety may be uncomfortable, but they are necessary emotions just like happiness and excitement. These emotions are simply there to give you information. Your brain is on high alert to protect you. Rather than get carried away by it, simply acknowledge what your brain is trying to do. None of what we are experiencing is comfortable, but it is where true change begins.

I am an action-oriented person, and when something is wrong, I want to fix it. Learning to sit with uncomfortable emotions and not do anything about them has been a tough nut to crack. Although the urge to fix the situation or run from the emotion is still there, I can now recognize I'm feeling sadness, or whatever emotion I'm feeling, and that's okay. I have started paying attention to my body, recognizing what I am feeling and where I am feeling it. Mind Over Moment is about simply sitting in that feeling without judging it or trying to change it.

It's normal to feel anxiety and fear in the middle of a pandemic. Hell, I'd be worried if you didn't feel some discomfort during times of tragedy. That doesn't mean you have to marinate in it. Feelings are fleeting and constantly changing.

Let's put this to the test. Moments ago, as I was going through the last round of edits on this manuscript, I got a call from Evan's therapist, Cody. "I called to let you know that Evan had an episode. After he broke a window, he tried to use the glass to cut himself, and I had to physically restrain him."

I was literally editing the part of the book that talks about embracing negative emotions at the very moment I got the call. Jay and I talked with Cody, learned more about the situation, and now I'm back at my desk.

Here's the thought process going through my mind as I try to talk myself through this. What emotions am I feeling? I'm angry, sad, scared, and disappointed. Where do I feel it? My chest feels tight and my breathing is shallow. My eyes are welling up with tears. I take a few deep breaths.

These feelings aren't enjoyable, but I have to sit in this for a few moments. Running from these emotions will only magnify the intensity and duration. Before building these skills and habits, I would have tanked for the rest of the day. I would have curled up on the couch in the fetal position, cried for hours, and second guessed myself as a mother.

This isn't to say that I won't have those days, but as I'm sitting here typing (writing helps me process really heavy emotions), I realized I was holding my breath. With my hands resting on the keyboard, I take three deep breaths and think, "Is it a shitty situation?" Absolutely. "Is there anything I can do at this moment to help Evan?" Nope. Evan is in a safe place with trained staff and therapists that care for him and will help him through this. He will recover, process the event, and move on. Sadness, anger, disappointment, and fear are normal reactions and part of the package when you have a mentally ill child.

Then I talk to myself in a positive and nurturing way. Talking to yourself in third person helps take you out of your limbic system and brings you back into your prefrontal cortex. I say, "Anne, you are strong. You have worked hard to be able to have Evan in a program that can provide the level of care he needs. At this moment, Evan is safe, and so are you."

I begin thinking of the things I am grateful for. I am grateful Evan is safe. I am grateful I didn't have to witness this episode as I have so many others. I am grateful Jay is here and we can support each other. I am grateful the sun is shining because the rain would only make this worse. I am grateful my dogs are next to me, and no matter what happens today, they will love me. I am grateful Evan didn't hurt himself. I am grateful Evan's therapist really cares for him and took the time to call us.

Practicing Mind Over Moment has allowed me to process this rather than revert to old habits that would only exacerbate the problem. I could numb the discomfort, but what would I have accomplished?

I debated sharing this because it is very personal, and I'm navigating in real time. I also know strength comes from struggle, and if I can help one person not end up in the fetal position on the couch, it's worth it. These strategies are the way I will get through this, and every time I get back up, I get back up stronger.

Proactively Cultivate Positive Emotions

While negative emotions are necessary, resilient people also make a concerted effort to proactively cultivate positive ones.

When I was in my first semester of college at the University of Kansas, I was so homesick. I remember telling my roommate that everything would be so much better if I were home. She looked at me and said, "Well, you take you with you wherever you go." Wait, what? All these years later, the moment is still so vivid in my mind.

I hear so many people say, "If only I had a better job, home, spouse, etc., I'd be so much happier." Unfortunately, if you're not happy where you are, there's a very good chance you won't be happy where you're going. The same "issues" seem to surface wherever you are and whomever you're with. You are the common denominator.

> *"If you're not happy where you are, there's a very good chance you won't be happy where you're going."*

Although it's certainly easier said than done, the secret is finding contentment where you are, who you're with, and with what you have before looking for more.

Resilience is built through proactively cultivating positive emotions to offset your negativity bias. It's also a key component to personal and professional success.

PRACTICE OPTIMISM

One of my favorite authors is Simon Sinek. I've read his books, watched his TED talk, spoken at a conference where he keynoted, and recently published an article in *Success* magazine that was placed on the page immediately after his. Simon has no idea who I am (yet), but now I can say, "Simon, I have your back" and mean it. When tackling the subject of optimism, he said, "Optimism is not wearing rose-colored glasses. Optimism is the belief that things will get better. That we will find a way to get out of it."

"Optimism is not wearing rose-colored glasses. Optimism is the belief that things will get better."

I think sometimes it is easier said than done when you're in the middle of it, but choosing optimism means you are deliberate about the way you interpret the adversity in your life. Every situation, especially the cruddy ones, provides an opportunity to learn something. And this isn't just fluff. Scientific research has proven that when you look at life through a lens of positivity, you are more likely to enjoy better mental and physical health.[33] When you attune your attention to the good things, you find more of them because you find what you look for.

My husband jokes that I'm the most pessimistic motivational speaker he's ever met. If I'm not deliberate (Mind Over Moment), I have a natural tendency to look at the negative side of things. A few months ago, I called him from the airport and said, "Well, I think I'm going to miss my flight." He gave me the usual pep talk, "Come on honey! Think positively!" I followed up with, "Okay, I'm positive I'm going to miss my flight!"

People often ask how I stay so motivated. Trust me, there are no unicorns farting rainbows in my bedroom, doves are not released when

I walk into a room, and I am not outside high-fiving sunbeams. It is a choice; sometimes hour-by-hour, and sometimes moment-by moment—and I don't always get it right. Resilience is getting back in the saddle after a slip.

Proactively working to cultivate gratitude, appreciation, optimism, and humor is a skill, and it will change your brain for the better. You can choose how you look at your life and the world around you. The other day, Evan called and said, "Mom, guess what! I have like $1,000 in savings!" I said, "Honey, you have $6 saved." He responded, "Exactly! I only have $994 to save until I get $1,000!" Your outlook is everything.

> *"Proactively working to cultivate gratitude, appreciation, optimism, and humor is a skill, and it will change your brain for the better."*

Optimism lowers cortisol and increases dopamine and serotonin. People who practice optimism have fewer aches and pains, along with better physical and mental health. It has also been linked with higher income and more successful relationships.[34]

Optimism doesn't mean that you ignore the reality of your situation. It's about choosing how you interpret the events in your life. Crappy things happen to good people every day. How you choose to interpret those experiences plays a big role in your ability to be resilient.

A week after Evan left for Idaho, Jay started building shelves high up in the garage. It had been impossible to get home projects done because we were always on alert and almost always exhausted. That day I had flown home from a week-long speaking event in Europe, pulled in the driveway, stepped out of the car, and heard Jay yelling for help. He was lying on the garage floor and had just fallen eight feet off a ladder.

Are you f#@%ing kidding me? In that moment, I went through every possible emotion. I was worried, pissed off, scared, frustrated, and more.

It was 104 degrees outside. Why the f#@% was he in the garage, on a ladder, eight feet off the ground, alone? Was this the universe's way of kicking us while we were down? What was happening? After Jay's motorcycle accident in 2013 (holy hell, we have been through a lot), he was not allowed to get injured again.

I called 911, the neighbors ran over, and within minutes a fire truck with six hot firemen flooded my garage. "Choose your perspective, Anne!" This was my chance to practice Mind Over Moment. Because humor is my greatest coping skill, I looked at Jay, looked at the firemen, and said, "Um, hey guys. I think he'll be okay. I, however, am feeling a bit faint. Which one of you would like to start mouth-to-mouth?"

Okay, so it may not have been the best timing, but it gave all of us, even Jay, a chuckle. Jay's broken hip, arm, and ribs may have made that chuckle just as painful as the fall.

When talking to friends and family, I caught myself saying things like, "I know! Can you believe it? If it's not one thing, it's another. Why do bad things keep happening to us?" Without realizing it, I was proactively cultivating negative emotions.

Seligman created the "3Ps of Resilience," which says three things can hinder recovering from adversity:

- **Personalization:** A cognitive distortion that makes a person believe they are to blame for every problem or that it is all about them. A person should take responsibility for a failure, but they should not see themselves as a failure.

- **Pervasiveness:** The belief that an event will affect all areas of our life instead of just one area. People who have this mindset can easily feel hopeless and overwhelmed.

- **Permanence:** The belief that your feelings or this situation will last forever.

Seligman found that your ability to recover from adversity is in large part determined by the way you view the adversity itself. You can build resilience simply by shifting the way you think about the situation at hand.

"Your ability to recover from adversity is in large part determined by the way you view the adversity itself."

Did I want Jay broken and hurting? Of course not. But I can look back with perspective and realize that it forced him to be still and to process all the things that were happening with Evan, something he would not have otherwise done. Did I want Jay to fall off a ladder? No, but it brought me and my daughter closer together as we cared for him side by side (and had plenty of laughs! Men can be such babies when they are hurt!). This was not permanent, it wasn't pervasive, and it certainly wasn't personal.

Adversity, and how you deal with it, builds character and resilience. Seligman suggests that when something bad happens, whether it's a tragedy or an inconvenience, you should:

- Describe the event as unemotionally as possible. Leave out judgment and evaluation.
- What is your belief about the event? (Not what you think your belief should be, but your default belief and interpretation.)
- What is the outcome of those beliefs? What action results?

If those outcomes or results aren't the ones you want, it's time to shift your interpretation.

CHOOSE GRATITUDE

"I am so tired of being appreciated! If someone else gives me a compliment, I quit!" said no one. Ever.

Although humans may be hard-wired to search for danger and identify threats, developing the capacity to search for the good stuff is also a fundamental skill we can add to our toolkit to thrive at work and at home. Gratitude has been proven to be the single best predictor of well-being and a strong determinant of resilience.[35]

People who practice gratitude have improved sleep, mood, decision-making, relationships, lower blood pressure, fewer aches and pains, fewer bouts of depression, and the benefits are almost immediate. A study from the University of California San Diego's School of Medicine found that people who were more grateful had better heart health.[36]

> *"People who practice gratitude have improved sleep, mood, decision-making, relationships, lower blood pressure, fewer aches and pains, fewer bouts of depression, and the benefits are almost immediate."*

You don't even have to find anything to be grateful for. The simple act of looking releases the feel-good neurochemicals serotonin and dopamine and lowers the stress hormone cortisol by 23 percent.[37] Looking for the good stuff attunes your brain to the positive. Gratitude is closely linked to your sense of well-being and makes you more resilient in the face of adversity. Expressing gratitude reduces toxic emotions, diminishes depression, increases happiness, and enriches relationships. You find what you look for, so look for good things.

Research shows that when you think about what you appreciate, the parasympathetic or calming part of the nervous system is triggered, and that can have protective benefits on the body and the brain.

Developing gratitude is an incredibly effective way to deal with stress, increase your ability to handle tough challenges successfully, and release yourself from living and working reactively.

SAVOR DELICIOUS MOMENTS

One way I practice gratitude is something I call a "delicious moment." We search for happiness like it's a destination, and when we don't find it, we feel like we have done something wrong. Happiness isn't the absence of negative feelings. Just like sadness, anger, fear, and frustration, happiness happens in micro-moments. Emotions are not a constant state, and just like the weather, if you wait it out, they will change. You can increase the likelihood of positive emotions by taking time to savor them. Every time you sit in a positive moment, you embed it more deeply into the neural structure of your brain.

We typically run past delicious moments, not even aware they are happening because we are searching for a constant state of "happy" that just isn't attainable. In our search for happily ever after, we miss the beautiful, happy moments, and a collection of those is what makes a beautiful life.

Whether it is savoring the first sip of coffee in the morning, gasping for breath after a wonderful laugh, or a hug from a friend, delicious moments are all around you if you just take time to experience them.

"In our search for happily ever after, we miss the beautiful, happy moments, and a collection of those is what makes a beautiful life."

Taking Evan to get a haircut used to be a huge ordeal, even a traumatic one. It often took several people to hold him down or keep him distracted. Never underestimate the power of a sensory integration processing disorder. A haircut is a sensory overload.

This particular haircut was a bit different. Earlier in the day, my first *Harvard Business Review* article had been published. This was a big career milestone and something that had taken a considerable amount of time and effort. What do you do when you have a career milestone? Post it on Facebook, of course.

Evan sat down with Annie at the Great Clips we have gone to since he was three. Annie knows our situation, so anytime she cuts Evan's hair, she has me sit in the chair across from him just in case he gets upset.

As soon as Evan was seated, I checked Facebook. How many likes and comments had my article received? I was searching for that dopamine hit. I looked up halfway through the haircut and realized that Evan was talking to Annie (in a volume appropriate tone—amazing!), he was giggling, and he was happy.

Rather than soaking that up and appreciating it, I almost missed it because I was busy checking my Facebook feed. After that, I started paying attention to the moments I wanted to savor.

One evening, we somehow convinced both kids to play that game where you put a giant plastic thing in your mouth and try to decipher a phrase. They should have a drooling warning on that game. We laughed hysterically! It was one of the most beautifully delicious moments. Another night we played cards and Rylee, who is a masterful choir singer, was singing along with a Selena Gomez album. I just soaked it in, searing that memory into my brain. The other night, Jay and I danced in the kitchen, celebrating a magazine article I just wrote, and I relished every second.

Delicious moments are everywhere and happen all the time, we are often just too busy to notice. Look for these moments and pay attention to them. Feel grateful for them. Savor them.

As Rick Hanson, a psychologist, leading resilience researcher, and author of *Hardwiring Happiness* explains, the more time you spend savoring these moments, the easier it becomes to find them.[38] Savoring is your ability to step outside of your experience to review it and appreciate it while it's happening. I have built a "delicious moments board" in my office. On it are pictures, letters, cards, sticky notes, cocktail napkins, etc. Every time I catch myself savoring a delicious moment like laughing until my stomach hurts, I write it down or take a picture of it and put it on my board.

> *"Savoring is your ability to step outside of your experience to review it and appreciate it while it's happening."*

Yesterday I left the house and realized I had forgotten my phone. I drove back home and went upstairs to look for it. After a few minutes of searching, I asked Jay to call me. I heard my Knight Rider ringtone and started feverishly trying to find my phone before it stopped. No such luck. Jay called me again, and again I ran around like a crazy person trying to find where the sound was coming from. It wasn't until the fifth try that I realized *the phone was in my back pocket* the entire time! We laughed hysterically, and I wrote it down and posted it on my board.

Not only does experiencing delicious moments increase dopamine and serotonin, when you go back and think about those moments later, it has the same effect. Whether it's keeping a gratitude jar, savoring delicious moments, or simply acknowledging them, when you take time to notice the positive, you train your brain to start looking for it.

Feeling gratitude is the first step, but expressing gratitude is the game changer. During my speeches, I often ask people to text someone in their life, thanking them for something specific. After one event, a mom came up to me and showed me the text exchange with her daughter:

Mom: Hi honey. I was just thinking about you and wanted to tell you how much I love you. You are the best daughter anyone could ask for.

Daughter: What's wrong? Are you dying?

Mom realized that she should be telling her daughter she appreciates her more. Take time to tell the people in your life you care for them, love them, and appreciate them. We often think it's assumed, but you know what they say about assuming.

BUILD A GRATITUDE HABIT

Gratitude helps you overcome fear, negativity, stress, anger, anxiety, and all those other pesky problems generated by an overactive amygdala. Hanson explains how to use "positive neuroplasticity" to remap your brain so you can feel more calm, content, and confident. And you can do it by weaving gratitude throughout your daily experience. He shares these examples:

- Instead of walking around your house looking at the mess your partner left, look for something that reminds you of how you appreciate your partner.

- Instead of criticizing your kids, find ways to celebrate their strengths.

- When the phone rings and you feel at the end of your rope, consider that your boss, coworker, client, or customer is calling because they value you and need your help.

Try this formula for putting the power of gratitude to work in your life:

- **Look for it:** Take a few moments throughout each day to identify things, people, and circumstances in your life for which you feel grateful.

- **Savor it:** When you have a delicious moment that sparks gratitude, take a couple of deep breaths, and focus on experiencing that moment and feeling.

- **Express/communicate it:** Expressing gratitude is contagious and increases dopamine and serotonin for both the person giving and the person receiving the feedback. It's an easy way to give another person a boost and lift your own spirits in the process.

Just like any other repeated thought pattern or behavior, gratitude can become a habit. Last year, our team created a gratitude challenge. People from all over the world sent us their gratitude list. Some were grateful for their health, others for an accomplishment, and many were grateful we were having a gratitude challenge. We collected all these responses, drew a name, and gave away a $250 gift card or a donation toward the winner's charity of choice.

> *"Just like any other repeated thought pattern or behavior, gratitude can become a habit."*

Now, here's the back story. I am embarrassed to admit it, but hey, gotta keep it real. I ordered the jar online, and when it arrived, it was much larger than I expected. It was huge! The first thing I said when I took the jar out of the box was, "Holy shit! How are we ever going to fill that jar?" Jay wrote a message for me and taped it inside the jar: "I am grateful I have such a big jar to fill." Did we fill the jar? Of course, we did! And a whole lot of people experienced joy because of it.

I even asked the kids to take part in the gratitude challenge. Rylee came home grumpy after a tough day. I told her about the gratitude challenge and asked that each day, she write something down that she was grateful for on a piece of paper and put it in the jar. The next day she came home and said, "UGH! I had to spend the entire day looking for something to be grateful for!" My response was, "Yes love, that's the point." She gave me a sly smile and a reluctant nod, letting me know she got it.

You can also habit stack. If there is something you do every day (like brushing your teeth), add a gratitude habit to it. When you brush your teeth tonight, think about something positive that happened during the day, something that made you smile, or just be thankful you still have your own teeth.

FIND HUMOR

One of my favorite things in the world is laughter. If you can't find something to laugh at, you aren't paying attention. Half the time I laugh at myself. On my last trip before the coronavirus, I was briskly walking through the Atlanta airport with carry-on luggage, and while there was absolutely nothing in my way, I managed to trip over my suitcase and fall flat on my butt. Ten strangers and I had a great laugh. I was laughing because I was embarrassed. The other 10 people laughed because I was laughing. We all laughed together and for a brief moment, it didn't matter who we had voted for, what religion we practiced, or the color of our skin. We all shared a good laugh together. Laughter is a universal language.

I have the unique opportunity to work with some very diverse organizations and people. A couple of years ago, I spoke in upstate New York to a group of hospital volunteers and auxilians. There were about 200 people at this conference, and not one was under 65 years old. Some of these folks were in their 80s and a few in their 90s! These sweet people worked at hospital gift shops, information desks, and as candy stripers.

The night before an event I have my little ritual. I treat myself to room service, get some work done, and lounge in bed. Although I sometimes go to dinner with the client, I usually prefer to chill and hang out in my room. There was no room service at the hotel, so at about 7:00 pm I wandered down to the lobby to find something to eat.

As soon as I got off the elevator, I was greeted by a woman who totally reminded me of my Grammy, a 94-year-old spitfire who still volunteers at the hospital twice a week. She hurried right up to me and said, "Dear, you must be lost. You are supposed to be at our trivia night."

She grabbed my arm and ushered me to the table right up front. I was seated with seven ladies who were laughing so hard, I thought we might lose one of them. They were cackling like my girlfriends and me after several cocktails. Apparently, our table had been battling with a rival team several tables back.

The next question was asked, everyone at my table was brainstorming, and one of our rival team members said something hilariously snarky to Ruth, a woman at my table. I learned that Ruth had just battled breast cancer and had had a double mastectomy. In response to the snarky comment, Ruth yelled back (at the top of her lungs and in a thick New York accent), "Suck it, Suzanne! If you're not nice to me, I'm not going to tell you where my new nipples are!" Ruth was Joe Pesci from *My Cousin Vinny*," if Joe Pesci were a woman.

I damn near fell out of my chair. I laughed so hard, I think I peed a little. Everyone at my table was hysterical, and the rest of the room followed suit. Ruth had dropped the mic and brought the house down in the process. Side note: I have a sticky note that says, "Suck it, Suzanne!" on my delicious moments board. It was too good not to remember.

Ruth and Suzanne had figured out what science has known for years: Laughter really is the best medicine. Studies show a genuine smile (one that involves facial muscles around the eyes) sparks a change in brain activity related to a good mood. A simple smile, even if it's initially a forced effort (or a side effect of a cosmetic procedure like Botox),[39] can reduce stress, improve your mood, strengthen your immune system, and help add a few years to your life.[40]

*"A simple smile can reduce stress, improve
your mood, strengthen your immune system,
and help add a few years to your life."*

Finding ways to laugh at challenges, stressful situations, and even personal tragedy is one way resilient people cope and grow through misfortune. It broadens your focus of attention and helps you face your fears while fostering exploration, creativity, and flexibility in thinking. Being able to laugh at challenges provides distance and perspective, but it does so without denying pain or fear; it manages to present the positive and negative wrapped into one package.[41]

Dr. Murray Grossman, an ENT (or otolaryngologist—go ahead, try to pronounce that) with Cedars-Sinai Medical Center and Torrance Memorial in Los Angeles, explains, "Just the physical act of smiling can make a difference in building your immunity. When you smile, the brain sees the muscle activity and assumes that humor is happening."[42] This means that your brain doesn't care why you're smiling—as evidenced by the Botox research—it processes the benefits of the smile regardless of its purpose.

I am part of a support group with other moms who have kiddos like Evan. Dark humor becomes a serious coping mechanism when you are dealing with things most parents could not fathom. We make jokes about our situation because humor is our saving grace. One day at breakfast one of the moms said, "I had a dream last night that Bobby got hit by a bus." Without missing a beat, she followed with, "I was driving the bus!" We roared with laughter and scared the people at the next table.

How is it that the mere act of smiling can change our mood? The answer to this question explains why practicing mindfulness helps reduce harmful reactions to stress and is one of the best ways to build resilience.

PRACTICE MINDFULNESS

Mindfulness means focusing your attention on experiences in the present moment without judgment—paying attention on purpose. Although the idea of mindfulness stems from Buddhism and other spiritual traditions, it is not a religion. This 2,500 year-old practice was first introduced in the western world in the late 1970s and has grown in popularity ever since.

If you think of exercise as strength and health for your body, mindfulness is strength and health for your mind. Contrary to what I used to believe, mindfulness does not require you sit in a full lotus position, eat tofu, or find your Zen. It is simply being where you are when you're there. Mindfulness trains your mind to focus on the moment instead of worrying about what occurred in the past or what might happen in the future. Practicing mindfulness helps you to become aware of your feelings, emotions, and experiences without judgment. If thinking of it in a spiritual sense isn't comfortable for you, think about it as brain training. You are training your brain to direct your attention where you want it to go. This awareness makes you less likely to hit the panic button.

*"Mindfulness is strength and health
for your mind."*

Mindfulness has been shown to lower inflammation, improve mood, help you sleep better, increase your ability to maintain attention, reduce anxiety and depression, manage chronic pain, and even reverse stress-related changes in the brain.[43]

If you are like me, you may still be skeptical. How can bringing yourself back to the moment change your brain, your health, and everything in between? Because we spend so much of our time in a frenetic state, training our brains to be still gives us tremendous power. The reason it is so effective lies in the connection between body and mind.

The vagus nerve has been called the "body's communication superhighway." It carries sensory information between the brain and internal organs, providing primary control of the parasympathetic nervous system that controls rest and digestion. About 10 to 20 percent of these nerve cells send commands from the brain to control muscles that move food through the gut, while 80 to 90 percent carry sensory information from the stomach and intestines to the brain. This explains the expression "I feel it in my gut."[44] Any time you experience any feelings or sensations in your body, chances are it's the vagus nerve—whether it's a broken heart, anger, or happiness. You know that you feel like this because your body has sent signals to your brain.

The vagus nerve doesn't just control digestion—it also controls rest and relaxation. The Scottsdale Institute for Health and Medicine explains the role of the vagus nerve in reducing stress when you practice mindfulness: "When the vagus nerve receives the signals from these meditation effects, it sends a message to the brain that all is well, there is no danger and there is no need to be in fight or flight. The brain then sends the message to the autonomic nervous system which stimulates the parasympathetic branch to come out of fight or flight and regulate the systems into balance."[45]

When you mindfully focus your attention on what you are experiencing in the moment, including your breathing and other sensations, you reestablish the calming connection that becomes frayed when stress triggers your fight-or-flight reflex. This is why mindfulness works, and why it is the basis for Mind Over Moment.

"When you mindfully focus your attention on what you are experiencing in the moment... you reestablish the calming connection that becomes frayed when stress triggers your fight-or-flight reflex."

Mindfulness can be as simple as catching yourself in hysterical laughter and soaking in the feeling, listening to the leaves move in the wind, or savoring the smell of bacon. You are practicing mindfulness when you notice thoughts, feelings, and sensations. The goal of mindfulness is simply to bring yourself back to the present moment.

Here is an easy mindfulness exercise called the five senses. Sit comfortably and take a few deep breaths. Then, breathe normally and identify five things that you can see. Notice the colors, shapes, sizes, and details. Next, think of four things you can feel. The fabric of your clothes touching your skin, the cool air on your face, your foot touching the floor, or the chair underneath you. Then, think of three things that you can hear. This can be the sound of a fan, someone walking down the hall, or the buzz of your computer. Next think of two things you can smell. Your wet dog, something cooking, or the perfume of someone sitting near you. Finally, notice one thing you can taste. Simply focusing on your senses brings you back to the present moment.

I was teaching a workshop on resilience in Canada, and one of the participants was the women's Olympic Canadian rowing champion. She introduced me to an exercise called "Take 5." Hold up one hand and with the index finger of your other hand, trace your fingers. Inhale as you move up your thumb, hold your breath when you get to the top of your finger, and exhale as you move down the other side. Then do the same with the rest of your fingers. When all is said and done, you've taken five deep breaths. She explained that the team does this before all practices and competitions to get focused.

The next time you find your thoughts racing, bring yourself back to the moment. Push your foot against the floor and feel the pressure on your leg. Eat a small piece of chocolate and taste it as it melts in your mouth. Take a few deep breaths. Simply bring yourself back to now.

I realize this sounds simple, and for a long time, I thought it was hokey. What you are really doing is training your brain to control your attention. We spend so much time judging our feelings, emotions, and thoughts, rather than just observing and sitting with them. This builds our emotional resilience and reduces reactivity.

TRAIN YOUR BRAIN WITH MEDITATION

One way to practice mindfulness is meditation. Like many people, I was looking for ways to relax and get out from under the mountain of stress that I felt. I was exercising, eating well, praying, and practicing gratitude, but I was still constantly reacting to a life that felt very much out of control.

People kept telling me to meditate, but I honestly didn't know what that meant. What do you mean I'm supposed to focus on my breath? Every time I tried to sit quietly and focus on my breath, it felt like I was playing whack-a-mole with my thoughts. My mind constantly wandered: "What are we going to have for dinner?" "I forgot to email Frank." "My leg itches. Why does my leg itch? Do I have a rash?" Screw it.

It turns out "focus on your breath" means just that. Focus on the sensation of the air entering your nostrils, the feeling as your chest and abdomen fill up with air, the sensation of blowing the air out of your mouth and exhaling. You've been breathing since the day you were born; you've just never given it much thought.

In fact, most of us breathe incorrectly. When we are stressed, our breathing becomes shallow, and we breathe from our chest. Diaphragmatic breathing is a technique that helps you take full breaths and sends a signal to your brain to relax. This breathing technique is so simple, it is easy to dismiss it. Take a deep breath in through your abdomen. You know you're doing this when you pooch out your stomach to make a Buddha belly. Then, hold for a few seconds and exhale as your stomach comes back in. This helps your brain get plenty of oxygen, and the exhale puts you back into your parasympathetic nervous system or rest and digest state.

What I didn't understand about meditation is that when your mind wanders, you know it's working. Meditation is not some Zen-like calm experience. It's hard work because your mind doesn't stop. Your thoughts will wander because your brain is always looking for something to grab onto (Buddhist monks aptly call this our "monkey mind"). Expect it and let the thoughts roll on by. Every time you bring yourself back to focus on your breathing, you train your brain to focus your attention where you want it to go. This makes you less likely to go off the rails when things go wrong and helps you be less emotionally reactive. A goal of meditation is to become aware of your thoughts and emotions as they arise, which helps you regulate and manage them.

"Every time you bring yourself back to focus on your breathing, you train your brain to focus your attention where you want it to go."

I try to start off the day with a few quiet moments. According to world-renowned meditation expert, Sharon Salzburg, the magic number is between seven and nine minutes a day. Meditating for seven to nine minutes a day will lower cortisol, reverse stress-related changes in your brain, and make you less likely to get carried away by your emotions.[46] Concentrating on your breathing is also a great way to calm your mind and fall asleep at night. I meditate to sleep every night.

There is no right or wrong way to meditate. Download an app, watch videos on YouTube, or simply sit quietly. Here is the practice I follow, but you should find the one that works for you.

MEDITATION 101

Sit in a comfortable position. Take a few deep breaths into your abdomen (inhale for four to five seconds, hold for four to five seconds, and exhale for four to five seconds). Then, breathe normally and do something called a body scan. I imagine a blue light starting at the tip of my head and slowly moving down my body, surrounding it, relaxing each part as it goes. I feel the light touch the top of my head, and I relax my forehead. That's about the time I realize I forgot to make a vet appointment for the dog or didn't call back my mother. That's okay. I observe that my mind has wandered and go back to my breath. The light continues down and slowly surrounds and relaxes my face, neck, shoulders, chest, arms, stomach, back, legs, feet, and toes, until my entire body is relaxed and surrounded by this warmth and light.

I sit and breathe normally, paying attention to my breath. Again, my mind wanders. I go back to my breath. The exhale is the part of your breath that brings you back to a relaxed state. I imagine a weight at the end of my exhale, going deeper into my stomach. Sometimes I don't catch my mind wandering until the time is almost up, and that's okay, too. This practice takes about 10 minutes a day.

Although this seems simple, it is really challenging and can even be frustrating, but each time you come back to your focal point (usually your breath) you are training yourself to control your attention, rather than letting it control you. When you practice directing your focus where you want it to go, and not where it gravitates naturally, you will change your life.

Mindfulness is a practice, and what you practice grows stronger. If you are practicing meditation while judging yourself and feeling frustrated, you are growing judgment and frustration. Don't worry about mastering these practices and just focus on doing them because it's the doing that changes you.

One of the simplest ways to practice Mind Over Moment is the "STOP" method developed by Jon Kabat-Zinn, creator of the Stress Reduction Clinic and the Center for Mindfulness in Medicine at the University of Massachusetts Medical School.[47] When you are feeling overwhelmed, he suggests following this acronym:

S: Stop whatever you're doing.

T: Take a breath—or better yet, three deep breaths. This resets your nervous system.

O: Observe what you are feeling and name the emotion. Rather than run from that emotion, pay attention to where you feel it in your body.

P: Proceed. Rather than ruminating over the emotion or what happened, give yourself permission to move forward.

The STOP method allows you to easily and instantly adopt a mindful approach to whatever you are doing. Mindfulness exercises such as this one, and other forms of meditation, train your brain to control your attention, and that is the goal.

Be Compassionate Toward Yourself

When was the last time you looked in the mirror and said something nice to yourself? In his book *Resilient*, Rick Hanson asks, "What would you do if you were on your own side?" He explains that most of us are a better friend to others than we are to ourselves.[48] Ain't that the truth.

"What would you do if you were on your own side?"

Think about it, how often would you talk to a friend the way you talk to yourself? We all have self-defeating, negative thoughts. Mind Over Moment is a tool to help you recognize when you aren't being kind to yourself. If you believe you deserve as much kindness and respect as anyone else, you can begin to shift those thoughts.

According to Hanson, the key to growing any psychological resources, including self-compassion, is to have repeated experiences that get turned into lasting changes in the brain. This means the more you practice self-compassion (or anything else), the easier it gets.

According to self-compassion researchers Kristen Neff and Katie A. Dahm, self-compassion means treating yourself with the same type of kind, caring support and understanding that you would show to anyone you cared about.[49]

They explain that self-compassion consists of three components:

1. **Self-kindness:** There are plenty of people who are kind and compassionate toward others but go for the total knockout when it comes to how they treat themselves. When a friend makes a mistake, do you berate her? Belittle her? Yell at her? Of course not. Then why in the world would you reserve that treatment for yourself?

2. **Common humanity:** Everyone fails, has missteps, makes mistakes, and gets things wrong. It is easier to practice self-compassion when you realize you are just like everybody else.

3. **Mindfulness:** This simply allows you to become aware that you are having self-destructive thoughts and emotions. Those who practice self-compassion don't replace negative feelings with positive ones; rather, positive emotions are generated by embracing the negative ones.

According to Neff and Dahm, one of the biggest findings of their research is that greater self-compassion is linked to less anxiety and depression. Practicing self-compassion has been found to deactivate the threat system in the brain, lower cortisol, and activate the ability to self-soothe.

It's no wonder that self-compassion is linked with strong emotional intelligence, life satisfaction, social connectedness, and greater physical and mental well-being.[50] Practicing self-compassion also builds the emotional resilience needed to cope with stressful life events such as divorce, health crises, academic failure, and even combat trauma.[51]

Self-compassion has been difficult for me. I am my own worst critic and sometimes I say things to myself I would never say to a friend. My therapist Sheerin suggested I name this self-critical voice to help separate it from reality. I have named mine Helga. I view Helga as this overweight, mean Russian woman wearing a dirty apron and carrying a rolling pin. Don't ask why because I have no idea. And if you are an overweight, mean Russian woman named Helga, I mean no offense.

Helga follows me everywhere, reminding me of every flaw, mistake, and mishap. I have the choice of choosing to listen to her or not. Giving a name to this voice has helped me because when I hear that self-critical, harsh voice, I know it's just Helga. She's negative and rude, and I don't want her in my brain house. Jay laughs because every once in a while, out of nowhere, I mutter, "Shut up, Helga!"

We are not used to practicing kindness and grace when it comes to ourselves, but building resilience requires that we start. Self-compassion builds empathy. After all, how can you truly be empathetic toward others if you aren't able to practice it for yourself?

Remember, your brain may not be able to make the leap from, "What is wrong with me!?" to "I'm awesome!" nor should it. But it can go from "What is wrong with me!?" to "All I can do is all I can do" or "It is what it is."

Self-compassion doesn't mean you don't work hard, hold yourself accountable, or challenge yourself, but it means that you do it from a place of kindness rather than self-loathing. We spend a ridiculous amount of time beating ourselves up, so much so that for many of us, it has become a habit. The next time you say something negative to yourself *about* yourself, stop, take a deep breath, recognize that it is just Helga (or whatever you choose to name your voice), and keep going.

Be Compassionate Toward Others

You're cruising down the highway, and as you approach your exit you realize that there is already a long line of cars waiting in the exit only lane. You would have gotten over sooner if you had paid attention, but you were lost in thought, and now you need to scoot over in order to exit. You glance at the driver next to you with that look of desperation only to see him inch right up to the car in front of him. You try to make eye contact with the woman right behind him. Surely, she will sense your embarrassment and be kind enough to let you in. Nope. This continues for a few more cars before you finally gun it, mumbling and cursing under your breath. Sound familiar? What were you thinking about the other drivers? Jerks! How rude! What is wrong with people!

But when was the last time you were one of the drivers, riding the bumper of the car in front of you, thinking "Like your time is more valuable than mine? I had to wait my turn in this line, and you should, too. Nope, not gonna do it."

Most of us can relate to being on both sides of this or a similar situation. If you are the one riding the bumper of the car in front of you, you have allowed yourself to become emotionally hijacked, causing a surge of negative energy, cortisol, and adrenaline. But is it worth it?

Kindness uses less energy than anger. Caring is easier than resentment. Peace is more comforting than battle.

Being kind to others—including yourself—will not only make this world a better place, but research shows it may also improve your overall physical health.

> *"Kindness uses less energy than anger.*
> *Caring is easier than resentment.*
> *Peace is more comforting than battle."*

- **Kindness keeps your heart healthy:** Studies have shown that being kind causes the release of oxytocin (and nitric oxide), which helps to expand your blood vessels and lower blood pressure.

- **Kindness makes you a happier human:** When you are kind, your body releases endorphins that may help to elevate your mood.

- **Kindness keeps you young:** Free radicals and inflammation, which are big contributors to the aging process, are reduced when you show love and kindness.

- **Being kind** has been shown to strengthen your immune system.

- **Kindness** truly is contagious.

Studies show that participating in random acts of kindness may encourage others to "pay it forward"—and the cycle continues.[52]

MAKE TIME FOR SOCIAL CONNECTION

I am so grateful for my tribe. I have some amazing friends, and I'm not sure how I would have survived this far without them. These are the people I call when I feel broken. These are the shoulders I cry on. These are my friends who catch me when I fall (and then laugh at me hysterically). Different friends ebb and flow through the course of your life, but if you are lucky enough, you will have a lifelong tribe who loves you to your core.

Friends become more important to health and happiness as you age. In fact, having supportive friendships in old age has been found to be a better predictor of well-being than having strong family connections.

"Having supportive friendships in old age has been found to be a better predictor of well-being than having strong family connections."

You are a collection of the people you spend the most time with. If you surround yourself with positive people, you are more likely to feel uplifted and happy. If you spend your time with people full of negativity and drama, you tend to see the world through that lens.

Social connection has proven to be one of the best predictors of longevity.[53] Surround yourself with people who lift you up, celebrate, and laugh with you. Surround yourself with people who embrace you and your imperfections.

Relationships take effort, and when you are tired or feeling down, it is much easier to isolate yourself. Resist the urge to withdraw and make an effort to stay connected to the people in your life that matter most. It can be a simple email, cup of coffee, or phone call, but if you don't make relationships a priority, you are sabotaging your ability to remain resilient.

Social connection and community drive resilience. This is why religious services are so powerful. In addition to the connection to something greater than yourself, it is a community of like-minded people.

Like optimism and gratitude, the happiness boost you get from connection with others is crucial to your health and well-being. Having friendships and a sense of belonging is considered a core psychological need and has a big impact on your physical health.

One study found that loneliness is toxic—it's more harmful to health than obesity, smoking, and high blood pressure.[54] People who are more connected to friends and family are "happier, healthier and live longer than people who are less well connected." They also enjoy better brain health as they age.

Humans are social creatures with emotional needs for relationships and positive connections to others. Our social brains crave companionship. We are not meant to survive, let alone thrive, in isolation.

During the coronavirus pandemic, depression and anxiety have increased dramatically, in large part due to social distancing. It is easy to forget that social distance does not have to mean social isolation. The real goal is physical distance with social connection.

Although you may not be able to share the same physical space with someone, virtual video connection is the next best thing. We feed off of the body language of others, so platforms like Zoom, FaceTime, and Skype that allow us to "see" those who are most important to us provide the happiness boost from connection with others that is crucial to our health and mental well-being, and a key element to building resilience.

Support groups have been one of the ways I have been able to survive this journey with Evan. I credit my support groups for helping me get through some of my roughest times. Studies have found that meeting other people who are further along in the same journey helps you to overcome permanence by showing you that you won't be stuck where you are forever.[55] Support groups connect you with others who really get what you're going through and provide human connection. The club that no one wants to be a part of provides incredible bonding.

When seeking social connection, be careful that you don't fall into the trap of social comparison, and social media makes this virtually impossible. When you see others' "perfect moments," it's easy to become disillusioned with your own life. When you compare your insides to their outsides, it's a recipe for disaster.

We use these comparisons to evaluate how we feel about our lives, relationships, and self. When I'm on Facebook or Instagram and see my friends with their adorable, sweet, compliant kids, it's easy to feel sad. It is a reminder of my reality. When you see friends' pictures of traveling the world, it's a reminder that you haven't been on vacation since Clinton was president.

Although social media is a great way to connect with people, it can often lead you to feel more isolated and alone. Don't compare your life to other people's highlight reel; you don't know what's happening behind the curtains, so to speak. Go on my Facebook page, and I can tell you the backstory of every single picture that I post. You might see a picture of me on a stage in front of thousands of people. I see that picture and remember crying before I got on stage because of something that happened with Evan.

Make time to connect with others. This might mean finding a new hobby, joining a gym, or roaming your neighborhood with a glass of wine until others join you. Do not go this journey alone.

The number of friends you have isn't as important as the quality of those friendships. Social connection doesn't mean you have to be an extrovert or love social gatherings. It is simply acknowledging that we need each other. Take time to connect with the people in your life.

During the coronavirus pandemic, I have had virtual happy hours with friends and connected with people I haven't spoken to in years. Sometimes it takes getting shaken to our core to remind us to prioritize our friendships and relationships. Send a text right now to someone in your life. Something as simple as, "I was just thinking about you" can be the little boost that person needs. The added bonus is that you feel good in the process.

HOPE IS A STRATEGY

There has been much in the news the last few years about how practicing gratitude is good medicine.[56] The research keeps piling up to show all the ways that being grateful boosts emotional and physical well-being, and protects you from depression, anxiety, high blood pressure, and other illnesses. Optimism and looking for the good in people and situations helps you live a longer and happier life. But what about hope?

Having hope and staying focused on a better future can sustain you when times are hard. I know this because I have never given up hope for Evan.

People often say hope is not a strategy, but it very much is. Having goals, being hopeful for the future, and celebrating small victories along the way builds resilience.[57]

"Having goals, being hopeful for the future, and celebrating small victories along the way builds resilience."

Several months ago, Jay and I traveled to Idaho to visit Evan for a weekend. He wanted to go fishing and took us to a bridge on a river in the most beautiful spot. It ended up being a calming, grounding, and peaceful experience for the three of us. Jay and I were amazed at how much better we felt after just an hour sitting in the fresh air and sunshine, watching Evan fish with a big smile on his face. Our hope had gotten us there.

It's wonderful when you see your hopes realized—and even more wonderful when that realization exceeds your expectations. Everyone has crappy days and weeks (and sometimes months and years) when everything seems to be going against them. It's those times when you most need to practice hope.

If you can't feel hopeful for yourself, sometimes you can bring hope to someone else who is struggling just as much or more than you are. Hope leads to positive emotions that help offset your negativity bias. When you feel anxious about the future, pause and think about what you *hope* will happen.

GET A HELPER'S HIGH

There's growing evidence that helping others benefits the giver as much as the receiver. A new study looked at how New Zealanders responded to help survivors of the Christchurch terror attacks that killed 51 people, including providing home-cooked meals, sending flowers, and offering other small acts of kindness. The researchers found these actions strengthened the resilience of those who performed them.[58] Kelly McGonigal, author of *The Science of Compassion*, calls this the "tend-and-befriend response." "Caring for others triggers the biology of courage and creates hope," she says.[59]

It helps you to help others. A 2005 review of research studies found that older adults who volunteer experience lower rates of depression, lower mortality rates, higher self-esteem, and greater functional ability than those who don't.[60]

When you give to others selflessly (not expecting anything in return), your brain releases dopamine, serotonin, and lots of other happy hormones that make you feel warm and tingly inside.

Of course, no one is 100 percent selfless, but one study shows that human brains are actually hard-wired for empathy and generosity. Our brains contain mirror neurons, the cells in our brains that allow us to understand other's actions, intentions, and feelings.[61]

I was speaking at a conference and running late. There was a Starbucks in the hotel, and just like the Hulk who you won't like angry, you won't like me without coffee. I figured I could get a quick cup of black coffee, nothing fancy and nothing time consuming. I walked up and a woman was in line before me. She started asking questions: "What is a pump? What is whip? What size correlates to a medium." Normally those questions wouldn't bother me, but I was in a bit of a hurry, and every question was like nails on a chalkboard.

I interrupted and said, "Excuse me. I'm running a bit behind and just want to order a black coffee. I'm happy to pay for your drink if you don't mind me grabbing one first." The barista gave me my black coffee, I left a tip and charged my drink and whatever she bought to my room. I thought I was off for the races, but the woman started to cry. My impatience has gotten the best of me before, and I felt horrible that I had made this woman cry! I promptly apologized, to which she said, "I'm crying because today is my birthday, and you are the only person in the whole world who got me a present. You just made my birthday special." The hairs stood up on the back of my neck, my eyes watered, and we hugged. I didn't make her day. She made mine.

Whether it is a small gesture like holding the door for someone, or a large gesture like building a house, every time you help others, you feel the benefit.

When Evan was in the hospital the first time, we lived at the Ronald McDonald House for two months. I have never experienced anything like it. Volunteers made three hot meals a day, we received Christmas presents for both kids even though Rylee was in Austin, and an anonymous donor covered the cost of our room for two weeks! It was only $15 a night, but when you are paying more for your medication than your mortgage, every little bit helps. That experience humbled me and reminded me how much good there is in this world.

I donate a portion of my book proceeds to National Alliance on Mental Illness (NAMI) Central Texas. They use this money to offer free resources, classes, support groups, and so much more. Although I love being able to do this, it's also selfish because it feels so good to know I am giving back. If you purchased this book, you have just helped someone.

Right now, the coronavirus is in full-swing, and while there is no shortage of pain and suffering, the stories of human kindness are overwhelming. Healthcare workers, first responders, and essential workers are putting themselves at risk to help those who are sick. Neighbors are stepping up to help each other in ways I've never seen before. CEOs are foregoing their salary so they don't have to lay off their employees.

On the news this morning, there was the story of a family who lives outside of Dallas in a small town called Waxahachie. This small family business has developed a face mask that hooks directly to an oxygen machine that reduces the need for ventilators, potentially saving thousands of lives and millions of dollars. With the help of a few doctors from around the country, they were able to make modifications to the mask to help with the coronavirus pandemic.

They wanted to reproduce the masks but didn't have the capital to purchase the equipment. Within 24 hours, Richard Branson, founder of Virgin Airlines, stepped up and saved the day.

Not only is this family keeping the cost of the mask the same as it was before the virus, they are giving the design away for free to any company that has the capability to reproduce it. The family has friends from their church volunteering 16 hours a day to help produce these masks because they know they will save lives.

There is so much good in this world. You are surrounded with beauty and love; you just have to let it in.

TAKE CARE OF YOUR MOST VALUABLE RESOURCE

You can't be kind to yourself if you aren't taking care of yourself. I can't tell you the number of times people told me to make sure I was taking care of myself when circumstances in my life were intense. I thought sure, in between running a business, raising two kids, being a wife, balancing friendships, volunteering, and more, I'll go ahead and take a spa day.

It turns out when you don't take time to stop and care for yourself, life has a way of doing it for you. In my case, I ended up with a tumor in my salivary gland that was the size of a small avocado. Removing the tumor resulted in facial paralysis. Because of the facial paralysis, I couldn't close my eye and a speck of dust scratched my cornea. I wore an eye patch, and because of my lack of depth perception, I fell down a flight of stairs and broke my foot in four places just before I started six weeks of radiation for the tumor. Yes, life has a way of stopping us in our tracks if we don't take time to do it ourselves.

I learned that self-care isn't selfish. It is a requirement for resilience, and it doesn't have to be a spa day. There are hundreds of little ways you can care for yourself every day.

"Self-care isn't selfish.
It is a requirement for resilience."

When you are tired and overwhelmed, you are at your most vulnerable. It is at these times when it is easy to revert to old habits that often sabotage your success.

Make caring for yourself a priority. I know this may go against your nature, particularly if you are a hard-driving, high-achieving person. If you are like me, you are constantly pushing yourself harder, and it goes against your nature to stop. Stop anyway.

When it comes to taking care of yourself, take the advice you would give your kids or your friends. It may be exercise, meditation, regular time with a friend, snuggling with a pet, taking time to read for fun, or dancing around in your underwear while jamming out to music. Don't neglect what brings you joy—make it a ritual and part of your resilience-building routine. You can't be a source of strength for others when you are depleted, and you can't be a spark for others if one is not lit in you.

Exercise Works

Exercise is one of the best ways you can care for your mind and body. I'm not one of those people who gets a runner's high and can't wait to go jogging. Those people make me twitch. But exercise has become a non-negotiable for me. I was diagnosed with clinical depression when I was 19-years old (I know—a depressed motivational speaker—the irony). Every doctor, therapist, psychiatrist, and spiritual guru I met with told me to exercise, and I fought it tooth and nail for years. Going back to Grammy's advice, if enough people tell you you're tired, it's time to lie down.

"Exercise is one of the best ways you can care for your mind and body."

I got so low and desperate at one point, I finally followed the advice and started swimming. Although I don't crave going to the pool to swim laps, I now crave the feeling I get when I'm done. I feel pride, strength, and health. Most importantly, when I swim regularly, my mood is dramatically improved. When I travel, I try to visit the hotel gym or do yoga in my room. Even 10 minutes a day builds health, strength, and resilience.

A study by Duke University found that 30-minutes of brisk exercise three times a week is just as effective as drug therapy in relieving the symptoms of major depression in the short term, and medical center research has now shown that continued exercise greatly reduces the chances of the depression returning.[62]

Depression is a serious mental illness and is typically treated best by a combination of therapy, medication, and self-care. Trust me, I'm on everything but roller skates. That said, exercise has helped me tremendously. It allows your brain to repair neurons damaged by stress; lowers the risk of Alzheimer's or other types of dementia and heart disease; produces changes in the parts of the brain that regulate stress and anxiety—and the list goes on.

The World Health Organization recommends adults do at least 150 minutes of moderate exercise, or 75 minutes of vigorous exercise, each week.[63] The great news is that research shows that you don't have to do it every single day; you can cram it all into two days and still get the same health benefits from it. Aerobic exercise like running and swimming appears to be the best for brain health.

You don't have to run marathons, do ultra-triathlons, or swim the Atlantic to make dramatic improvements in your cognitive ability and resilience. This morning I sat in my office and debated going swimming. "It's cold, I'm tired, I'll do it later today, etc." I had some really great excuses. Then, I practiced Mind Over Moment. Swimming was something I could do to help me feel better, think better, and behave better. My excuses couldn't do those things.

Since undergoing radiation treatments, I can't turn my head in the pool. I get bad headaches and neck tightness, so I swim with a snorkel. I look like a total dork. On the upside, it allows me to meditate underwater. I focus on my breathing as I swim each stroke. My mind may race to something else, but breathing and feeling the sensation of gliding through the water with each stroke brings me back to the present.

Yoga is another exercise I've recently started. I subscribe to Yoga with Adriene on YouTube. She's cool and laid back (and happens to be in Austin), and she has made yoga accessible for me. I'm not great at it, and I can't do any cool tricks...*yet*.

Even if you just use it for stretching, yoga is so good for you. Plus, it gives you a twofer: it combines exercise and meditation, so it helps your brain that much more. My favorite part about yoga is that when I do downward dog, my dog Charlie does it also and kisses my nose. His downward dog is way better than mine.

Too much psychological stress causes inflammation in your body, and that is what causes aches and pains. Mind-body activities like yoga have been found to decrease signs of inflammation, which can help reduce the chronic effect of stress on the body.

Another bonus of exercise? A recent article in the *Journal of Applied Psychology* found that people who burned more calories daily were less likely to take out their anger about work issues on the people they lived with, compared with those who moved less.[64]

There are certainly times that I have an overwhelming urge to hit someone—in the face, with a chair. I credit exercise because I have yet to do that. #Winning.

Sweet Dreams

I love sleep. I mean, I really love sleep. One of my favorite parts of the day is crawling into bed at night, at least when I'm at home. I travel a lot and after watching one of those *Dateline* specials where they go to the hotel with a black light to see what's really in the bed and on the walls, I'm not so crazy about crawling into hotel beds. Apparently, even the fancy ones are nasty. Ick.

In Ariana Huffington's book, *The Sleep Revolution*, she explains that "we are in the midst of a sleep deprivation crisis, with profound consequences to our health, our job performance, our relationships and our happiness."[65] In fact, it is such a detriment that according to the Centers for Disease Control and Prevention:

> Sleep disorders are so pervasive in the United States that they now constitute a public health epidemic. Research conducted by the CDC indicates that many Americans experience problems associated with lack of sufficient sleep. For example:
>
> ■ 23.2 percent of survey respondents (almost 50 million people) reported problems concentrating during the day.

- 11.3 percent (24 million) indicated lack of sleep interfered with driving.

- 8.6 percent (18 million) reported that sleep deficiency interfered with job performance.[66]

According to this research, "sleep disorders represent an increasing risk to public health, contributing to a host of medical conditions, including cancer, obesity, diabetes, depression and hypertension."[67] Poor sleep leads to higher levels of anxiety and stress, and that impacts your ability to stay resilient.

I know how compelling it is to watch one more episode on Netflix or send that one last email. I even know how tempting it can be to do some online shopping at 3:00 am. I also know that if you want to practice Mind Over Moment, you must give your brain and body the resources they need to do it.

There are thousands of books and articles written on the topic of improving sleep. Suggestions include going screen free for an hour before bed, stretching, taking a warm bath with lavender oil, practicing progressive muscle relaxation, and so many more.

Every night, I lay down and make a conscious effort to slow my breathing. This gets me out of the sympathetic fight or flight nervous system and back into the parasympathetic nervous system. Then, I meditate and do a body scan, going back to my breath every time my mind remembers something I forgot to do, worries about things I can't control, or overthinks something I said or did. Then, I go back to my breath and keep going.

*"Don't underestimate the importance of sleep
or its role in helping you build resilience."*

I sleep better than I have in years, and if I wake up in the middle of the night, I meditate to go back to sleep. It has truly been life changing. Don't underestimate the importance of sleep or its role in helping you build resilience.

TOOT YOUR HORN

Reese Witherspoon, actor, activist, and women's champion, was the keynoter at an event where I was speaking. She really is as adorable as she seems, and she is also incredibly intelligent. She asked everyone in the audience to close their eyes and think of the dirtiest word you could think of. I cuss like a sailor, so my mind went straight to some doozies. She had us open our eyes and then said, "How many of you thought about the word 'ambition'?" Not a single person. Then she said, "since when did ambition become a dirty word?"

Advocating for yourself at work and home is also a form of self-care. Not only are you allowed to toot your own horn, it's your responsibility. Self-promotion isn't sleazy, it is simply communicating your value. The next time you finish a project, take a moment to send an email to your boss, copy your team, and thank everyone for the time and effort they put in.

> *"Self-promotion isn't sleazy, it is simply communicating your value."*

Keep a list of completed projects, successes, and new skills. When you have a performance review, share it. Use one-on-ones as an opportunity to discuss career development and succession planning.

Practicing mindfulness is not the opposite of ambition; it is your success accelerator. Whether you want to create a new product, start a business, write a book, go for a promotion, start a new career, or learn how to cook, practicing these strategies will help you get there faster, with greater ease, and more mental clarity.

Remember, you are in charge of your career and your life. Life is too short, and you spend way too much of it at work for you to be unhappy. It's tough to build resilience when you're going through the motions, just holding on for retirement. You deserve more.

PRACTICE STRATEGIC STOPPING

Strategic stopping is the most basic form of self-care. It means rather than living out of your inbox or reacting to the next emergency, you take control of your day. Taking regular breaks at work, including lunch breaks, has been shown to help reduce burnout and improve your focus and engagement.[68]

It might be tempting to take a quick break to check out your latest social media updates or do some online shopping, but it is easy to lose track of time and get sucked into whatever interests you. If you look up and 30 minutes have gone by, that wasn't a strategic break—it was a distraction that just chomped a big hole in your day. It's also a quick way to get emotionally hijacked.

Surfing the web may distract your brain, but it does nothing for your body. You need physical movement to do that. At least once an hour (and more often if you can), stand up, stretch, and take a few deep breaths. Go outside, take your dog for a walk, or take care of a physical chore. Taking a break for physical activity resets your mind and improves focus and creativity.

The point of strategic stopping is to give your mind time to recharge. It could be as simple as lighting a candle and watching the flame flicker or taking 15 minutes to do something creative, even if it's just doodling. Daydreaming has a bad rap, but it is a great way to rest your brain. Chris Hemsworth hangs out in my daydreams all the time.

"The point of strategic stopping is to give your mind time to recharge."

One way to strategically stop is the Pomodoro Technique, a time management strategy developed in the late 1980s. Just like High Intensity Interval Training (HIIT), this technique is based on working for short bursts and taking frequent breaks.

I use this method when I'm writing. Because writing requires a large amount of focus, I will set a timer for 45 minutes. At the end of that time, I get up, stretch, snuggle the dogs, take a few deep breaths, and go back to work. There are now entire apps and websites dedicated to incorporating this technique into your daily routine.

Strategic stopping can be as simple as deliberately choosing to focus on one thing at a time, then the next. Pause and be deliberate about the choices you face in each moment, large and small. If you think you don't have time, think again. The reason you can't is the very reason you need to.

Allowing your brain uninterrupted time to relax increases creativity, improves problem-solving, and provides stress relief. A study by Harvard found that clearing your mind for 15–20 minutes a day can literally change how your body functions at a molecular level.[69]

Develop Your Skillset

Emotional intelligence, gratitude, mindfulness, self-compassion, helping others, and self-care are just a few of the skills that can build resilience. Remember, it's not enough just to change your behaviors. You might be "doing" all the right things, but if your mindset isn't supporting your actions, you won't get the results you're looking for.

Do not try to tackle all these skills at once. Too much change all at once equals no change at all. Remember, baby steps. If all you can muster is a daydream with Chris Hemsworth, bravo. You have taken a step toward building your resilience.

Part Three:
RESET

In part one, you explored your mindset, your toolbox, and the foundation for building unstoppable resilience. Part two included tools that you can use to proactively cultivate the habits, skills, and behaviors that build resilience. Now it's time to learn how to reset. A reset is your ability to regain control, focus on what is most important, and create the life you want on purpose. A reset is about perspective.

SWIM TOWARD YOUR LIGHTHOUSE

It's easy to get carried away being busy, reacting through life, and not achieving what is most important to you. Many of us spend all week looking forward to the weekend, only to realize that we fill those days catching up on all the things we didn't get done during the week. By Monday, we need a weekend to recover, and then we hold on for dear life until we get to repeat the cycle all over again. Remember Penelope, the little gerbil who ran on her wheel but never got anywhere? This is your chance to break free of The Penelope Syndrome.

For more than six years, we had an in-home caregiver to help with Evan. Michael is from Tanzania and has such a calming presence. After an episode or a difficult interaction, Michael would literally send us to opposite ends of the house and tell us all to reset—to start fresh. He reminded us to focus on what is important: our family, love, health, future, and priorities.

This is hard to do when you are exhausted and emotional, but just like anything else, the ability to reset is a habit.

I swim in a pool that has lines painted on the bottom to keep me headed in the right direction. If you have ever tried to swim in a straight line in open water, you know that it is impossible because you are constantly being moved by the tide and current.

Most people I meet think, "If I just keep my head down and work hard, everything will fall into place." The problem is that if you just keep your head down, focused on what's next, you will end up where you are headed without realizing you may be going off course. For some people, moving with the current is a good thing. They like taking each day as it comes, never knowing what tomorrow will bring. There is absolutely

> *"If you just keep your head down, focused on what's next, you will end up where you are headed without realizing you may be going off course."*

nothing wrong with that approach, and there are many days where I wish I were laid back enough to live my life this way. I prefer to aim for a destination.

It doesn't mean I don't veer off-track from time to time, but when I do, it is a choice I am intentionally making.

If you swim in the ocean or other open water, you are taught to aim for an immovable object, like a buoy or a lighthouse. That way, regardless of where the current moves you, there is something steady to aim for.

Life is very much like the ocean. There are some days where the sun is shining, birds are chirping, and the seas are calm. Enjoy the crap out of those days. Other days you get shit on by a seagull and there are storms with crashing waves that will suck you under. When you come up for air, if you don't have anything to aim for, it's easy to get swept away.

Anytime I want to reset, I aim for my lighthouse. It is the calm in the storm that keeps me moving in the right direction. I have little lighthouses that I look forward to, like a vacation or date night. But other lighthouses are bigger. These lighthouses guide me, my decisions, and my daily behavior. I don't always swim in a straight line, and there are definitely days where the current gets the best of me, but I head toward my lighthouse nonetheless.

PICK YOUR LIGHTHOUSE

Last year was our tenth wedding anniversary. Having kids, especially one with special needs, makes it difficult to take a vacation. So other than taking a few short trips, we really hadn't had the chance to get away. We decided to spend a week in Antigua (pronounced "an-tee-ga"...who knew?), and this became a lighthouse we swam toward for an entire year. We planned, saved, and dreamed about this trip.

After months of anticipation, and one travel debacle after another, we finally made it there. As soon as we checked into our room we walked onto the balcony, and there, off in the distance right in front of us, *was a lighthouse*! We literally found our lighthouse. We spent the next week laughing, snorkeling, sailing, jet skiing, eating, drinking, and having the best time of our lives. Having a lighthouse gives you the motivation and determination to get to where you want to go.

We endured torrential storms and crashing waves on our way to this lighthouse. When you are trying to navigate the tough times, having something to aim toward and look forward to helps make the choppy water a little more bearable, and that builds resilience. Your brain is looking for ways to help you swim in the right direction regardless of all the other things that are trying to suck you under.

"When you are trying to navigate the tough times, having something to aim toward and look forward to helps make the choppy water a little more bearable, and that builds resilience."

One of my bigger lighthouses is mental health advocacy. As I continue to grow my business, I make decisions with that in mind. I want to reduce the shame and stigma of mental illness. As someone who has struggled with depression, I can attest that the stigma is real. You wouldn't shame a diabetic for needing insulin, and you shouldn't feel shame if you struggle with mental illness. Nonetheless, people do and refuse to talk about it. I swim toward my lighthouse so I can change that.

What are some lighthouses you can swim toward? What's off in the distance that you can look forward to and get excited about? I have a girl's weekend once a year with my tribe. That is a bright and shining lighthouse. Hell, pizza night can be a lighthouse. A lighthouse is anything that keeps you headed in the right direction, and that journey begins by defining success.

DEFINE SUCCESS

What does success look like for you? After all, if you don't know what success looks like, how are you ever supposed to achieve it? Like George Harrison said, "If you don't know where you're going, any road'll take you there." If you don't know your goals, how can you determine if any activity is a better use of your time than another?

*"If you don't know where you're going,
any road'll take you there."*

If you have ever been to a financial planner, they ask how much money you will need after retirement to live comfortably, and then they work backward. The same is true for life and success.

It's time to reverse engineer your life. What is it that you want? More time? Money? Friends? Rest? There is no right answer, but if you can't answer that question, you will continue to get carried away by the current.

No one has a perfect definition of success, nor do they flawlessly execute a path to get there, but without some idea of where you want to end up, you will stay busy being busy. If you are thinking, "I will know it when I see it," think again because that's not how your brain works. When you give your brain a destination, it subconsciously works backward to build the path to get there.

I was teaching a career development class for one of my corporate clients. The group was made up of high-potential up-and-comers, all under age 30. I asked them to take a moment to define success. Some answers involved a title: success means being a CEO. For others it was a happy, healthy family (which used to be mine, but when your family is not happy or healthy, does that by definition make you a failure? I sure as hell hope not!). And for one young lady, the answer was "happiness." I don't fault her for wanting to be happy, but happiness is not a constant state, nor should it be. You can't appreciate the good times if you never have bad times. Defining success with a feeling runs the risk of being fleeting, unpredictable, and unsustainable.

Some people define success with money as their measuring stick; others use status. If you want to ensure your unhappiness, find someone who is doing better than you and compare yourself. For many, success means freedom and flexibility. I caution people who say, "When I get _____, I will be successful and happy," because anything you can get, you can "unget."

It's easy to say, "I'll be happy when...," but the truth is, happiness doesn't depend on a destination. Happiness isn't a personality trait or a pot of gold at the end of a rainbow. Happiness is a skill. Remember what my wise roommate in college said: if you aren't happy where you are, you won't be happy where you are going.

> *"Happiness isn't a personality trait or a pot of gold at the end of a rainbow. Happiness is a skill."*

Daniel Goleman and Richard Davidson explain, "true well-being flourishes from the inside out. We can't chase it, and we can't buy it. But we can train ourselves, mind, body, and heart, and grow the 'muscle' that enables our best selves."[70]

Interestingly enough, I'm not even sure it's happiness that we really want. I would argue that what most people want is equanimity. Goleman defines equanimity as "a form of happiness that is not dependent on external circumstances." Practicing this belief system allows you, and only you, to determine your happiness.

If you could design your life (which you can), what would you want it to look like? This requires you to get out of reaction mode, and that is where Mind Over Moment comes in. One step toward creating the life you want is to make a dream board. Cut out pictures from magazines or find online images of things you want to achieve, places you want to go, people you want to meet, and anything that excites you. When I was going through facial paralysis, I cut out an image of a huge smile. After my face healed, I posted a picture of a big stage, envisioning myself standing on it. And now I have pictures of an RV because Jay and I want to travel the country and drive to speaking gigs. If you can't see it, it is hard to believe it. What pictures will go on your dream board?

Unfortunately, a vision with no action is not likely to generate the outcome you want. There is no success without hard work, grit, determination, and effort. But all the grit and determination in the world won't help if you don't know what you're aiming for.

SUCCESS IS A HABIT

Success is more than a destination. Success is a collection of habits, a way of living, and a routine, for lack of a better word. There are hundreds of books and articles that outline what the most successful people do every day. If you want to be successful, whatever that definition is for you, you have to think and behave in ways that will get you there.

"Success is more than a destination. Success is a collection of habits, a way of living, and a routine."

For starters, what information do you consume? If you are spending countless hours watching the news, it is easy to believe that everything in the world has gone to hell in a handbasket. War, poverty, and suffering become your reality. I'm not suggesting you don't keep up with current events, but what are you consuming to offset that?

There are countless podcasts, books, articles, meditations, comedians, and feel good shows that can offset some of that negativity. The most successful people choose to consume information that supports the life they want to live and the goals they want to achieve.

What is your success routine? If you stay up late to finish that last episode on Netflix, snooze your alarm for an hour in the morning, and roll out of bed exhausted, you are going to have an uphill battle. The problem for most of us is that instead of making subtle changes, we try to change everything at once.

Let's say you decide to go to bed earlier, wake up at 5:00 am to go for a run, eat tofu and bean sprouts, and meditate for an hour each morning. Unless you do most of those things already, the chances that you can sustain those things all at once are slim to none.

Need help figuring out where to start? Remember, baby steps. You don't have to get it perfect because this is a practice. Here are healthy habits that will set you up for success, whatever that definition might be for you:

- Get seven to eight hours of sleep each night
- Eat a healthy diet
- Stay active and exercise
- Spend time with friends and family
- Volunteer
- Plan and prioritize your day
- Practice self-compassion
- Learn something new
- Meditate
- Set a goal
- Practice gratitude
- Pray
- Read, watch, and listen to inspirational messages
- Journal

A success routine allows you to slowly adopt habits that cultivate success and give up things that are undermining it. I get it, it sounds easier said than done, which is why you can't do it all at once.

PAY ATTENTION TO YOUR PRIORITIES

I'm willing to bet you spend time most days prioritizing your schedule. Whether you have kids, pets, family obligations, or any number of things going on, it takes time to figure out how to make it all work. Prioritizing your schedule is important, but how often do you take time to schedule your priorities?

Resilient people make time for things that fill their bucket because it's impossible to be resilient with an empty one.

Practicing Mind Over Moment means that you take time to stop and pre-determine how you are going to invest your time. Invest is the operative word. Time is one of the few resources you can't get back or make more of. Everyone has the same 86,400 seconds in a day, and if you aren't deliberate about how you spend those moments, they will get filled with whatever is screaming the loudest for your attention.

"Resilient people make time for things that fill their bucket because it's impossible to be resilient with an empty one."

If taking time to relax is your intention, then you can relax without feeling like you should be doing something else. The goal is to be deliberate and intentional about how you spend your time. Start by tracking your time for a week and look for patterns. If after lunch, you get sucked into an hour of cat videos, that may not be the best use of your time. Everyone needs downtime and brain candy, so I'm not suggesting you abandon cat videos all together (there are some pretty hilarious ones out there), but if you find yourself procrastinating by doing things that are sabotaging your success, it's time to re-evaluate your priorities.

As someone who is very career- and goal-oriented, I have had to learn a very important lesson: Your eulogy and resume should not be the same thing. No one is going to stand over your grave and say, "She worked 80 hours a week. Hell yeah!" Your work is an important *part* of your identity, but it is not your identity. We are working ourselves into a slow grave. According to research at Ohio State University, women whose work weeks averaged 60 hours or more over three decades appeared to triple their risk of diabetes, cancer, heart disease, and arthritis.[71]

> *"Your eulogy and resume should not be the same thing."*

In the middle of the pandemic, my step-mother passed away, and I wasn't able to travel to the funeral. When I spoke to my dad he said, "Annie, I've got some harsh news—you are going to die…eventually. What do you want in your obituary? You have a unique opportunity to write it now and work backwards."

What do you want your dash to stand for? The Dash is one of my favorite poems. It is about the hyphen between the year you were born and the year you die and how you choose to live your life. Every day I wake up breathing is a good day. I might not enjoy every moment of the day, but I want my dash to count.

What do you wish you had more time for, and where is it scheduled on your calendar?

WORK/LIFE BALANCE IS NOT THE GOAL

Yesterday after work I volunteered at a homeless shelter. Then I went to the gym and had a great high intensity workout. I got home, showered, and cooked a beautiful meal for my family. After cleaning the kitchen, I baked cupcakes for the school fundraiser, and of course they were non-GMO and free of gluten, dairy, nuts, and soy. And because I still had a ton of energy, I had a romantic night with Jay.

Who am I kidding? Yesterday after work I passed by a homeless man and gave him a granola bar that had been in my car for God knows how long. I drove by the gym, but it looked hard, and I didn't feel like getting sweaty. I swung by the Chick-fil-A drive through and picked up dinner because, hey, chicken is healthy. I forgot I was supposed to make cupcakes, so I stopped by the grocery store on the way home and picked up two dozen dairy-, peanut-, gluten-filled cupcakes and didn't even take them out of the original packaging. After all that, I looked at Jay and said, "not tonight, honey." Then I passed out.

How do some people have it so together? Do they have a secret password or a special key that gets them into their perfect world? Although it might seem like Carol from accounting has her act together, everyone is really just hanging on for dear life! There are family dynamics that cause anxiety, obligations and last-minute tasks to finish at work and home, kids out of school who need to be entertained, and financial pressure weighing on our shoulders. Throw in a healthy dose of self-judgment for where we might have fallen short and we beat ourselves up.

"Define your true priorities and spend most of your time there without apologizing for it."

We compare ourselves to an impossible standard and then shame ourselves when we can't meet it. In my book *52 Strategies for Life, Love and Work*, I wrote about the idea of a "balance wheel," a way to divide your time to create balance. The irony is that I also had a chapter titled

"Forget the Idea of Balance." I don't believe your goal should be balance; instead, it should be to define your true priorities and spend most of your time there without apologizing for it.

Rather than the balance wheel I once used, now I use a self-care sheet so that I can consciously devote time to the things that matter most: family, friends, finances, physical and mental health, personal development, etc. At the end of each week, I have a glass (or four) of wine and set goals for the following week. I'm joking! *It's vodka.*

Sometimes, I focus on one goal in a singular area, and sometimes I focus on more than one. For example, a few months ago, my "lighthouse" was to spend time with family and friends. I had been traveling a lot for work, and I wanted to reconnect with Jay, the kids, my extended family, and friends. I made a plan to spend quality time with our kids, meet friends for brunch or dinner, hang out with my mom, and scheduled date night. Simply making an intention of putting a focus on this area helped make it a reality.

SELF-CARE SHEET
USE THIS CHART TO SET YOUR GOALS EACH WEEK.

PHYSICAL HEALTH	FAMILY	MENTAL HEALTH
1.	1.	1.
2.	2.	2.
3.	3.	3.
FINANCES	SOCIAL LIFE	CAREER
1.	1.	1.
2.	2.	2.
3.	3.	3.

As it turns out, a pandemic of epic proportions helped to solidify this plan. After being at home for more than five months, I'm ready to get back on a plane!

Where in your life could you use a little time and attention? What people, activities, and experiences could you schedule time for on your calendar?

If your goal is to get a handle on finances, how much can you realistically save each week, and what will you do to either earn extra money or spend less? How will you track progress? If you are focused on health, when have you scheduled time to exercise and cook healthy meals?

Getting clear on your priorities doesn't take away busy, but it ensures that you stay true to what's most important despite it. Each week make an intention to focus on something or someone that is important to you. Then, let the rest of your week fill in the gaps.

A couple of years ago, I spoke at a conference that featured Michelle Obama (a total career highlight). Although the Secret Service didn't do a full-blown body cavity search, they did have to clear every single person who entered the room. By the time all 3,000 of us were seated, we had waited in line for more than two hours. And might I say, it was worth every second.

She began by saying that balance begins by believing you are worth it. She joked about being *that mom*, calling her daughters' school on the first day so she could get all the important dates on her calendar. She schedules time with friends, kids, exercise, etc. first and then puts everything else on her calendar.

As a working mom who travels a lot, I sometimes have to sacrifice one priority for another. Although I would love to attend every recital, sporting event, and school play, it just isn't realistic. Are there days when I feel guilty, cry, and get overwhelmed? Of course! Just like you, I am human. That doesn't mean I don't continue to try. Mind Over Moment means taking each opportunity on a case-by-case basis. You cannot be everywhere at once, and you cannot be all things to all people, but you do have choices. Even inaction is a choice.

Schedule time for what matters most. The rest will fall into place.

"Schedule time for what matters most.
The rest will fall into place."

Stop Searching for Your Passion

Speaking at the Peabody Opera House for TEDx St. Louis Women was one of the most memorable experiences of my life. It was a career milestone and a check off of my bucket list. I speak in front of a lot of audiences, and I always get nervous, but this was different. This was a whole other level of nervousness.

I was scheduled to speak last. While waiting for my turn, I sat in the audience and listened to the other speakers. I still remember physically shaking the whole time. I was shivering, nervous, and sick to my stomach. That was until Terri Trespicio took the stage. I met Terri the night before at the cocktail hour meet and greet for the speakers. I remembered her because I had seen her first TEDx talk about finding your passion, and I loved it.

She explained that we have this idea that we are supposed to find our "passion," but that "passion" is overrated. Her take is that feeling like we need to find that *one* thing is limiting and overwhelming, that we chase our passion to the exclusion of all else in our life. We believe if we just find and chase our passion, everything will fall into place. And if it doesn't, we have somehow failed.

I agree with Terri that passion is a feeling, not a plan. And feelings change. What you might feel passionate about at one moment, doesn't necessarily mean you will feel the same way the next. I'm passionate about cake, but I didn't become a baker. I'm passionate about my dogs, but I didn't become a veterinarian. And I'm passionate about talking. Hey, one out of three ain't bad!

There is so much pressure to find your passion, that you miss opportunities to explore other interests. Terri jokes, "You show me someone who washes windows for a living, and I will bet you $1,000,000 it's not because he has a passion for clean glass."

Do you think the guy who developed the squatty potty was passionate about sitting on the throne? Speaking of squatty potty, another one of my guilty TV pleasures is *Shark Tank*, a show about entrepreneurs who ask investors for financial investment in their ideas in exchange for part ownership in their company. The squatty potty got its major break on *Shark Tank*. Full disclosure: I have a squatty potty, and might I say, it is magical. One of the entrepreneurs was explaining how he decided to follow his passion when one of the sharks responded, "Everyone talks about following their passion. People should be talking about following their effort."

So true! We spend a lot of time talking about our passions, but do our efforts reflect that? Do the priorities and choices we make every day align to what we say is important to us and what we're passionate about?

"Everyone talks about following their passion. People should be talking about following their effort."

Let's say your dream is to start your own business. How much time do you spend thinking, dreaming, and talking about it versus actually doing something about it? I talked about writing my first book for six years before I finally did something about it. Being passionate is wonderful. Demonstrating effort that makes your passions a reality is even better.

If you can't find your one true passion, congratulations, you are like 99 percent of the population. It's the moments searching for what makes you feel passionate that count. Those are the blips of happiness to savor. Pay attention to what brings a smile to your face, energizes you, and makes you feel better about yourself. What types of things and people are you naturally drawn toward? When does your inner badass shine? There isn't one right answer and trial and error is part of the package.

Back to TEDx St. Louis. It was finally my turn to speak at the biggest event of my career. I was the only one who used a prop—a bop bag like I had when I was a kid. You punch it, and it pops back up. I thought this prop idea was genius. What I hadn't anticipated was that we had to fill the bottom of the bop bag with water, and my bop bag sprung a leak. Looking back, I can say it was hysterical, but in the moment, I was freaking out! Jay and the stage manager were feverishly wrapping the bop bag with duct tape, desperately trying to make sure it survived the next 20 minutes without deflating or spraying water on the audience. We finally got it wrapped up, the lights went down, and I took the stage.

The next 18 minutes were a blur. I watch the video now and don't even remember much of it. I made a mistake, re-arranged part of the speech, and slipped up a few times, but none of that seemed to matter. When I was done, 3,000 people launched to their feet and gave me a standing ovation. It was one of the most delicious moments I have ever experienced.

Then the adrenaline wore off, and I went back to my life. Sitting here at my keyboard right now, do I feel passionate? I certainly don't feel passionate right this second while sitting in my sweatpants and over-sized sweatshirt working on this book. Even if you love what you do, it doesn't mean you feel "passion" every single second.

Finding things you enjoy sometimes requires you to get out of your own way. It is easy to get so comfortable in your routines that you stop trying new things or getting out of your comfort zone. When was the last time you tried a new hobby or did something fun in your own town?

I have lived in Austin for 20 years, and last year was the first time I ever went to chicken shit bingo. Yes, it is a real thing, and it is freaking hilarious. Let me set the scene. People line up to purchase a number. A chicken is put on a table with a bingo board full of numbers, and there is seed all over the table. The chicken eats the food, and the winner is chosen when the chicken relieves itself on a number. Classy huh? I can now say with complete confidence that chicken shit bingo is *not* my new passion, but I had a blast figuring that out!

THE POWER OF PURPOSE

You are here on this planet for a reason. You have special gifts to offer the world. What will you do with this limited time that you have been given? What will you do to make your mark on the world?

I recently got a phone call from a woman named Staci. Staci has terminal Stage IV cancer. She saw me speak at a women's conference, and she wanted to know if I could help her tell her story to the world with the limited amount of time she has left.

Staci had been an Olympic figure skater and skated with Disney. After her first cancer diagnosis at the age of 21, Staci returned to her goal- and achievement-oriented life. After her second diagnosis, she did the same. It wasn't until the third diagnosis, terminal cancer, that she decided to make a change.

We spoke for almost an hour and she bravely shared her decision to live each and every day like it was her last. Since her diagnosis, she has traveled to Africa, Costa Rica, and across the United States to do the things she has always dreamed of doing.

Staci realized that she learned how to live by dying. Her renewed purpose is to share her story so that she can inspire others to start living before it's too late. I checked in with Staci recently and she contracted the coronavirus. Due to her weakened immune system, she had to stay isolated, away from her family. It would be easy for her to play the victim, but even after all she has gone through, Staci is still focused on moving forward, and she is a shining example of resilience.

Resilient people possess a clear sense of meaning and purpose that enables them to stay the course when things get tough. It's much harder to feel defeated when you have a deep sense of meaning for what you're working toward.

> "Resilient people possess a clear sense of
> meaning and purpose that enables them to
> stay the course when things get tough."

Along with passion, the idea of "finding your purpose" can be a little ubiquitous. You can start by doing things that are meaningful for you. In *Option B,* Sheryl Sandberg and Adam Grant write, "meaningful work builds resilience and helps buffer against burnout. On days when people think they've had a meaningful impact on others at work, they feel more energized at home and more capable of dealing with difficult situations."[72]

Having a strong sense of purpose in life has also been shown to benefit health, which naturally makes us more resilient. For instance, a study by Northwestern University and Rush University Medical Center found that older adults with a purpose in life sleep better.[73] The study found that "having a good reason to get out of bed in the morning means you are more likely to sleep better at night with less sleep apnea and restless leg syndrome." I don't know about you, but I've got enough problems. The last one I need is restless leg syndrome!

You don't have to quit your day job to pursue your passion and purpose. If you love to speak in front of people, look for stretch assignments or volunteer to lead a lunch-and-learn. If you gain energy from solving problems, ask your manager what his/her most pressing problem is and offer to help solve it. And if spreadsheets are your thing, go find some data that needs spreadsheeting.

You can practice Mind Over Moment simply by taking time to explore what is important to you and what interests you. How can you use your unique gifts to help others? Your purpose already exists within you. It's not something you have to create. You can start to live your purpose by living on purpose.

EMBRACE FEAR AND FAILURE

It's not your mistakes that limit you; it's your fears. Taking risks and being willing to fail builds resilience. Not only do you learn more from failure than success, you learn more from bigger failures because you take time to analyze, problem solve, and prepare better for the next time. When I look back over my life, most of my regrets are the chances I didn't take because I was scared, not the ones I took that didn't work out.

When it's safe to talk about mistakes, people are more likely to report errors and less likely to make them. Teams that focus on learning from failure outperform those that don't. It boils down to promoting growth instead of blame. When you are willing to fail, you have already grown.

Highly resilient people treat problems as a learning process. For them, "fail" stands for "first attempt in learning." They also see fear as "false evidence appearing real." Embracing these words empowers you to step outside of your comfort zone more frequently because even if you "fail," you know you'll learn from mistakes, which ultimately brings you closer to your desired outcome. How do you turn failure from a regret into a resource? By using challenges as an opportunity to acquire or master skills.

Building resilience means you must be stronger than your excuses. View failure as an essential, inescapable element of growth. The question is not if you will fail, but when you do, how will you learn from it and get better?

"Building resilience means that you must be stronger than your excuses."

TAME YOUR FEAR

How much time do you spend being fearful? I'm not talking about monsters in your closet scary, but how much time do you spend being scared of the unknown? It's much easier to stay comfortable with old problems than be fearful of trying new solutions. It's kind of like those old pajama pants with a hole in the crotch. You know it's time to let them go, but they are so damn comfortable, and who is looking at your crotch anyway?

Whereas some people embrace change and say, "If it's not broken, break it! We can make it work quicker and better!" others dread the idea of having to do things differently than they have done them before.

Want to know a secret? A little fear is a good thing. I'm often asked how I can get up in front of thousands of people and speak without being nervous. Um, what makes you think I'm not nervous? The trick isn't getting rid of the nerves; it's channeling the energy in the right direction. You need a little adrenaline boost every now and then. Instead of jumping out of a plane, I jump on a stage! (Side note: If you are in a business where you are on a stage, be very careful about how you communicate this to your children. When teachers used to ask Evan what his mom did for a living, he would say, "She goes to fancy hotels and they pay her when she gets off stage.")

It is said that 95 percent of what we're afraid of never even happens, and the other 5 percent are things we can't control. We spend an inordinate amount of energy focusing on the "what ifs" and worst-case scenarios. What is the best-case scenario? What will it look like when things go right?

If you're not uncomfortable, you're not getting better. You are here to grow and learn, and if you are always in your comfort zone, growth is not possible.

Rylee's first job was at Panera Bread, and she came home after her first four-hour shift and said, "I'm going to quit. I hate this job." When we asked why, she said "because I don't know how to do anything, and I feel stupid." We encouraged her to give it time, and within a few weeks, she was training new employees. No one knows what they are doing—until they do.

When things don't go as planned, use that experience to practice resilience by searching for opportunities for personal growth. Remember, failure is only bad if you're perfect.

LEARN FROM FAILURE

I don't know any highly successful people who haven't suffered setbacks throughout their life and career. All of them can name numerous failures. It's a fact. Successful people fail more than unsuccessful people. Successful people take risks, they view failure as a learning opportunity, and they practice resilience. They choose to use failure and adversity to learn and get smarter. J.K. Rowling, author of the much-loved and critically acclaimed *Harry Potter* series, said, "It is impossible to live without failing at something. Unless you live so cautiously that you might as well not have lived at all—in which case, you fail by default."[74] She was rejected by 12 publishers and had no idea that her path to failure would lead her to become the first person to become a billionaire just by writing books.

Walt Disney was fired for having "no imagination" and Steven Spielberg was rejected from the University of Southern California Film School—three times. Dr. Seuss was rejected by 27 publishers, Oprah was fired and told she was "unfit for television news," Colonel Sanders failed at almost every endeavor he tried until the 1,010th franchise he pitched to adopt his recipe (when he was 65 years old). The list goes on and on. Failure is not the opposite of success. It is a requirement.

"Failure is not the opposite of success.
It is a requirement."

I'm willing to bet that when you woke up today, you did not start the day by saying, "Today is going to be a great day to fail!" But maybe you should have. Failure equals learning. Every year, the Bill and Melinda Gates Foundation has a Fail Fest where they celebrate what they learned while investing money into organizations that ultimately failed. I see organizations tout that they encourage risk-taking and innovation, but if you are operating in a culture that will slap your hand if you fail, you end up operating in a threat state. The fear of failure shuts down the creative part of your brain. Your priority becomes protection instead of innovation.

If you don't have the luxury of failing at work, fail at home. Try a completely new hobby or activity. On our last trip to visit Evan, we had a family team building exercise at an indoor rock gym. I had never been to a rock gym, but it's basically a bunch of different walls with colored pegs that simulate rocks and mountains. You are supposed to use those tiny little pegs to scale the wall.

As I previously mentioned, I have never considered myself athletic, at least not *yet*. I gave it my best shot. I put chalk on my hands, stretched, and wore special shoes. Apparently, gravity was not my friend. I didn't only fail, I face-plant failed. It was awful! But you know what? I learned from that failure. I learned that I have courage to try something out of my comfort zone. I learned that rock climbing isn't for me (at least not yet). And I learned to wear a belt. I'm not sure what was worse, face planting or everyone seeing my butt after my pants fell with me.

Failure is uncomfortable and sometimes scary but recovering from failure (and doing it often) accelerates your ability to grow from your experiences. Every single time you recover from a setback, you get stronger as a result. Don't waste failure. Learn from it.

Actor Will Smith said, "Fail early, fail often, fail forward. You have to seek failure; it's where the lessons are. At the gym, you're seeking failure. That's where growth is. Extract lessons and use energy and wisdom to get to the next phase of success. You have to live at the edge of your capabilities. Live where you're almost certain you're going to fail. Practice is controlled failure, taking you to the limit. Failure helps you recognize the areas where you need to evolve."[75]

FEAR OF NOT MEASURING UP

Much has been written about the imposter syndrome. Imposter syndrome can be defined as a collection of feelings of inadequacy that persist despite evident success.[76] "Imposters" suffer from chronic self-doubt and a sense of intellectual fraudulence that override any feelings of success or external proof of their competence. "What if everyone figures out I don't know what I'm doing! I just got lucky. I really don't belong in this job."

I have dealt with imposter syndrome for my entire career. As someone who literally sells me for a living, rejection can be especially hard. It's easy to slip into social comparison and self-doubt. And I'm not alone. An estimated 70 percent of people experience these impostor feelings at some point in their lives.[77] Impostor syndrome expert Valerie Young, author of *The Secret Thoughts of Successful Women*, has also found patterns in people who experience impostor feelings, including perfectionists, who question their competence and ability with even the smallest mistake.[78] People who are naturally "smart" or "talented" often feel this way when things don't come as easily, or when they experience a setback. Then, of course, you have people who think if they just work harder than everyone, they can prove they are not imposters.

Rachel Hollis. Mel Robbins. Brené Brown. Marie Forleo. These are just a few of the incredibly successful speakers, authors, and entrepreneurs I admire. Although I'm not proud of it, I'll admit I have wondered, "What are they doing that I'm not?" and "Why can't I measure up?" This thinking creates seeds of self-doubt that can become quite paralyzing. Make no mistake about it, these feelings are totally normal, and I would venture to guess most people feel this way at some point. What you do about those feelings is what matters.

You are practicing Mind Over Moment when you realize that you are feeling this way. Simply observing the thought gives you an opportunity to choose whether you engage it. Just because that annoying self-doubt creeps in doesn't mean you have to listen to it. Observe the thought, recognize how you feel, and keep going.

> *"Just because that annoying self-doubt creeps in doesn't mean you have to listen to it."*

Remember the growth mindset? When I have one of those "not measuring up" moments, I remind myself that rather than waste effort and energy comparing myself to others, I can focus on becoming a better version of myself. Rachel, Mel, Brené, and Marie have skills that I don't have. *Yet.*

Fear can be paralyzing or motivating, and as an entrepreneur, I can completely relate. I was terrified to start my own business. For the longest time I tried to convince myself I wasn't starting my own business because I didn't want to, but when I really dug down and thought about it, fear was holding me back. After living at the Ronald McDonald house for two months while Evan underwent inpatient psychiatric treatment, I figured if I can do that, I can figure out how to build a business. Has it been easy? Hell no! Have I had multiple failures? Hell yes! And I've continued to learn, grow, and improve as a result. We can use fear productively.

The more you practice Mind Over Moment, the greater your self-awareness, and the easier it is to step outside of fearful and inhibiting thoughts and feelings and just observe them. You will begin to catch yourself in the middle of a self-defeating thought. Rather than engage in the thought, just begin to notice when you have it. It is simply there for information. There is no need to challenge it, change it, or do anything about it. It's just Helga. That is the beauty of mindfulness.

If you feel the need to take action, you can also manage fearful or anxiety-causing thoughts by going into problem solving mode. Is there something you can do to solve it? Can you learn a new skill? Take a class? Read a book? Practice? Thoughts become less scary when we realize they may just be problems that need to be solved.

Evan is beginning his senior year of high school, and I can feel the anxiety creeping in. "What will we do when he gets home? How will he hold down a job? Will we support him forever? What is the best living situation for him? How will we manage it all?" The list of thoughts that race through my mind seems unending. I realized that most of the anxiety is coming from the unknown.

Simply recognizing these feelings has been a big accomplishment. I would have normally allowed that anxiety to spiral, spilling out in unhealthy ways. Practicing Mind Over Moment has allowed me to realize they are just emotions, feelings, and information. Period. I can minimize the unknown by taking steps each day to learn what programs are available, talk with other parents who are further along in the journey, and approach it as a project, instead of an overwhelming and daunting task.

The same holds true for just about everything. You can use your emotional energy to worry and be fearful, or you can reserve that energy for the things you can control.

"You can use your emotional energy to worry and be fearful, or you can reserve that energy for the things you can control."

Vulnerability Makes Us Stronger

It is hard to embrace failure because it makes us vulnerable. In her book *Daring Greatly: How the Courage to Be Vulnerable Transforms the Way We Live, Love, Parent, and Lead*, Brené Brown defines vulnerability as "uncertainty, risk and emotional exposure."[79] Vulnerability, she says, "is the birthplace of love, belonging, joy, courage, empathy and creativity." All of those are building blocks for becoming more resilient.

In the past, the idea of vulnerability was usually associated with weakness. Being vulnerable meant being susceptible to being hurt; showing vulnerability was the same as showing weakness. In recent years, the word vulnerability has come to be used in a broader context—as in when you choose to share parts of yourself that you might be tempted to keep hidden. If you choose to be vulnerable with another person, that's not a sign of weakness. It's a conscious choice that requires courage.

After speaking engagements, people often come up to me and thank me for being vulnerable in sharing my story. It wasn't until recently that I became even more vulnerable. Although I shared Evan's mental health journey, I hadn't shared my own. Being a clinically depressed motivational speaker doesn't just roll off the tongue, but I've learned that rather than being ashamed, I am an advocate. I am more confident than ever that if these strategies and tools can work for me, they can work for you. Vulnerability is tied to trust, and trust is the keystone of strong and resilient relationships. Harvard Business School professor Amy Cuddy notes that when people first meet someone, they ask two questions: (1) "Can I trust this person?" and (2) "Can I respect this person?"[80] Respect is based on perception of competence, but only comes after trust is established.

> *"If you choose to be vulnerable with another person, that's not a sign of weakness. It's a conscious choice that requires courage."*

Vulnerability helps establish trust because it is how we share common humanity. In addition to helping humanize our work, it's a key element of courageous leadership.[81] Showing vulnerability by sharing our feelings, asking for help, or taking responsibility for a mistake can even make us more attractive to others. Researchers have coined this the "Beautiful Mess Effect."[82] I don't know about you, but I'm down for anything that makes me look more attractive and doesn't require surgery or duct tape!

Vulnerability can be scary. We crave certainty, and building emotional resilience requires you to get uncomfortable with ambiguity and the unknown. It means that you risk being hurt but are still willing to forge ahead into the unknown because ahead is the only way to go.

Mental Health Lessons from the Trenches

Raising a child who suffers from mental illness is the hardest thing I have ever done, and it truly tests the meaning of unconditional love. One in five adults and children struggle with a serious mental health problem in their lifetime, which means that every single one of us is impacted by this public health crisis.

It's easy to get angry with the people in our lives who suffer from mental illness. They can be irritable, forgetful, irrational, and difficult. Mental illness is isolating, overwhelming, and scary.

"One in five adults and children struggle with a serious mental health problem in their lifetime, which means that every single one of us is impacted by this public health crisis."

Unlike a disability that you can see and wrap your head around, mental illness is different. When I'm walking through a store and Evan is screaming at me, I feel shame and embarrassment. I imagine the other parents who are staring at us thinking, "What kind of mother allows her kid to talk to her like that?"

We live in a culture that isn't comfortable talking about mental illness, nor do we see it as the health crisis that it is. Although we are gaining traction, there is still a long road ahead to reduce the stigma that is attached to it. You can make a difference by being vulnerable, sharing your own experiences, and making it safe for others to share their experiences with you.

If this pandemic has taught us anything, it is that we are all interconnected. We might have different goals, outlooks, and priorities, but we are all going through life doing the best that we can.

If you are struggling and have made consistent efforts to improve your mental and emotional health and are still having trouble functioning optimally at home, work, or in your relationships, it may be time to seek professional help. There is *no* shame in admitting you or a loved one is struggling.

We have to make a concerted effort to protect our mental health because there are so many ways that everyday life takes a toll on our emotional well-being. We are taught to take care of our physical health, but mental health is just as—if not more—important.

If someone you love is struggling, share available resources, provide a safe space, listen, and practice patience. When friends or family are hurting, it is natural to want to fix it. When I'm going through a rough time and someone tells me I shouldn't feel sad because I have so much to be grateful for, or to look on the bright side, it just creates more guilt and shame.

As hard as it might be, simply be present for the people you love. Sometimes just knowing someone is out there who loves you and supports you makes all the difference. Unless you are a trained therapist, be cautious of offering advice. Everyone and their mother told me what I should do to make Evan "better." Although I appreciate that their advice is coming from a place of love, sometimes you just want someone to listen.

INCORPORATE MIND OVER MOMENT EVERY DAY

The older I get the faster time seems to pass. Some days seem to drag on, yet the weeks and months fly by. To paraphrase the great Ferris Bueller, if we don't take time to look up once in a while, we might miss something.

Life is made up of moments, and how you spend those moments defines you. You have an opportunity every single day to make those moments count.

Using Mind Over Moment doesn't have to be, and shouldn't be, a Herculean effort. Here are just a few of the things you can do to practice:

- Sit quietly for a few moments in the morning before launching into your day
- Deliberately look for positive moments and experiences
- Go screen free for 30 minutes before bed and after waking up
- Stretch
- Laugh
- Plan your day
- Read something uplifting
- Call a friend
- Exercise
- Rest
- Breathe slowly
- Meditate
- Take a walk
- Process emotions before responding
- Show compassion to yourself and others
- Express gratitude

Any time you are being deliberate about how you show up, you are practicing Mind Over Moment.

Embrace yourself as you are and your life as it is, without judgement. It is not perfect. It is perfectly flawed. Starting to hear that critical voice in your head? Mind Over Moment—you can decide not to listen to it. Getting carried away by your emotions? Mind Over Moment—observe the emotion and choose how to respond. Starting to feel overwhelmed? Mind Over Moment—take a few deep breaths and then move forward.

Building your resilience muscle proactively means living purposefully, rather than drifting into automatic. It's time to delve into your automatic thought patterns, belief systems, and daily habits to identify which ones are serving you. Resilience is built through deliberately cultivating productive thoughts and beliefs. Every habit you build (or let go of) is going to either serve you or not.

While you are on this journey, remember that everyone else is too. Give yourself and others grace by assuming positive intent. Sure, sometimes people are assholes, but more often than not, everyone is doing the very best they can. Someone cuts you off in traffic? Maybe they have diarrhea. A colleague throws you under the bus in a meeting? Maybe she is going through a messy divorce. Your kids seem to be intentionally pissing you off? They are struggling to fit in and keep up in school.

We all are just trying to find our way. Life is messy, yet you have everything you need to not only survive obstacles and adversity but get stronger because of them. Your scars are there to remind you of what you have overcome. And remember, every time you fall and get back up, you can add that to the database of things that did not defeat you.

"Every time you fall and get back up, you can add that to the database of things that did not defeat you."

If you want change, knowing what you need to do isn't enough. You also know you should eat right, exercise regularly, and get plenty of sleep. It's not enough to know the "what." You must also have a powerful "why." And until that "why" is so powerful that you are willing to be uncomfortable, don't waste the energy trying to change. Where you are has to be so painful that you are willing to be uncomfortable in order to change it, or where you want to go has to be compelling enough to make it worth the discomfort. What do you want, and what are you willing to do to get it? Do you want change, or do you want comfort?

When you are looking back on your life, what will you regret if you don't start making changes now? How will you challenge yourself to break through barriers keeping you stuck? What will you do differently tomorrow than you did today?

> *"Do you want change, or do*
> *you want comfort?"*

This is your time. No one else is going to do the work for you, and believe me, this is work. You can either spend your time repeating the same problems and patterns or make up your mind to choose this moment to take back control.

You will stumble, fall, make mistakes, do the wrong thing, and then you will get back up and keep going, only now you will be stronger and smarter.

Practicing Mind Over Moment has taught me so much, and I'm hopeful that these strategies and tools will do the same for you. I am begging you, please give yourself grace. Treat yourself as you would a close friend, and at the very least, with the same courtesy and respect you would give a stranger. We often treat strangers with more compassion than we offer to ourselves.

The coronavirus and the unrest that has followed has been a unique opportunity for the entire world to come together, fighting a common enemy and working toward a common goal. It is a shame that it takes something so drastic to stop us in our tracks, but it has stopped us, nonetheless.

As I sit here typing, the tree outside of my office window is blowing in the wind. The bright green leaves are blowing back and forth, and the branches are swaying with the strong wind gusts. Yet the tree stands firm, its roots deeply planted beneath the ground.

You may sway with the wind, have your branches shaken, and even lose some leaves along the way, but your roots are strong. Take comfort knowing that you have survived the worst thing that has ever happened to you, and you will continue to survive because you are a fighter.

CONCLUSION

Thank you for taking this journey with me. My hope is that you move forward, living a life of purpose, on purpose. Make time for what is most important because you never know how much time you have. Practice Mind Over Moment because after all, life is nothing more than a collection of moments. Make them count.

When you catch yourself sweatin' the small stuff, breathe. When you are angry or hurt, breathe. And when your dog vomits under your bed at 3:00 am, just go ahead and clean it up so you can go back to sleep in peace.

> *"Practice Mind Over Moment because after all, life is nothing more than a collection of moments. Make them count."*

Take time to celebrate how freaking amazing you are. I know that sounds cliché, but I mean it. Make notes to remind yourself that you are strong, write sayings on your bathroom mirror (mine says "I am enough" and "You got this") and make time for what is most important. Check out the *Mind Over Moment Journal* with prompts, exercises, and personal challenges to put what you've learned into action.

I'd like to leave you with a poem that I wrote while stranded in the Philadelphia airport for seven hours. Yes, seven hours. And although I did get frustrated every time they delayed my flight, I also practiced Mind Over Moment. There are worse places to be stranded than in a building with bathrooms and food, I would eventually get where I was going, and things ended up working out.

You, my friend, are full of goodness. Sprinkle that shit everywhere.

STRONG ENOUGH
By Anne Grady

When life knocks you down, and you're feeling defeated
When you're tired, overwhelmed, and your courage depleted
When you question your strength to get through the day
And your rose-colored glasses are now colored gray

Remember, discomfort is the birthplace of growth
You can choose courage, or you can choose comfort,
But you cannot choose both

You have pulled through tough times to get where you are
The strength that you have is because of those scars
So look toward your lighthouse and find moments to savor
You are now tougher, and smarter, and stronger, and braver

You have what it takes to survive times that are tough
You are courageous, you are resilient, and
YOU ARE STRONG ENOUGH!

I wish for you a lifetime of delicious moments!

About the Author

Anne Grady is not your typical motivational speaker. She is an entrepreneur, best-selling author, two-time TEDx speaker, survivor, optimist, inspirer, and truth-bomb dropper. Anne is a leading expert on resilience and leadership, contributing to *SUCCESS Magazine, Harvard Business Review, Entrepreneur, Fast Company,* and *FOX Business.*

Anne shares inspiring personal stories, cutting edge, research-based content, and implementation tools to transfer learning into real life to improve relationships, navigate change, and triumph over adversity. Audiences and readers love Anne's raw honesty, edgy humor, authenticity, and insight.

Her first two books are *Strong Enough: Choosing Courage, Resilience, and Triumph,* and *52 Strategies for Life, Love & Work.*

Anne lives in Round Rock, Texas, with her husband, two children, and their "therapy" dogs Bernie and Charlie.

For details on how to bring the strategies in this book into your conference or organization, contact Anne at hello@annegradygroup.com. You can also visit her online at www.annegradygroup.com and follow her on all of your favorite social channels @AnneGradyGroup.

NOTES

1 Irene S. Levine, *Mind Matters: Resilience*, American Association for the Advancement of Science, https://www.sciencemag.org/careers/2011/06/mind-matters-resilience.

2 Gratitude Is Good Medicine, UC Davis Health (November 25, 2015), https://health.ucdavis.edu/medicalcenter/features/2015-2016/11/20151125_gratitude.html.

3 Charles Duhigg, *The Power of Habit: Why We Do What We Do in Life and Business* (New York: Random House, 2014).

4 Carol S. Dweck, *Mindset: The New Psychology of Success* (New York: Ballantine/Random House, 2016).

5 Benjamin G. Shapero, Lyn Y. Abramson, and Lauren B. Alloy, "Emotional Reactivity and Internalizing Symptoms: Moderating Role of Emotion Regulation," *Cognitive Therapy and Research* 40, no. 30 (June 2016): 328–40, https://www.ncbi.nlm.nih.gov/pmc/articles/PMC4876867.

6 Agnese Mariotti, "The Effects of Chronic Stress on Health: New Insights into the Molecular Mechanisms of Brain–Body Communication," *Future Science* OA 1, no. 3 (November 2015): FSO23, https://www.ncbi.nlm.nih.gov/pmc/articles/PMC5137920/.

7 Chronic Stress Puts Your Health at Risk, March 19, 2019, https://www.mayoclinic.org/healthy-lifestyle/stress-management/in-depth/stress/art-20046037.

8 "The Big Life," *Women's Health* (April 2017), p. 149.

9 Kathleen Doheny, "How Long Work Hours Can Be Especially Bad for Women's Health," *Chicago Tribune* (June 23, 2016), https://www.chicagotribune.com/lifestyles/health/ct-long-hours-women-health-0623-20160623-story.html.

10 World Health Organization, Burn-Out an "Occupational Phenomenon": International Classification of Diseases, May 29, 2019, https://www.who.int/mental_health/evidence/burn-out/en/.

11 Kelly McGonigal, *The Upside of Stress* (New York: Avery, 2016).

12 Ibid.

13 Ibid.

14 Ibid.

15 Kelly McGonigal, *Making Stress Your Friend*, TEDGlobal 2013, https://www.ted.com/talks/kelly_mcgonigal_how_to_make_stress_your_friend?language=en.

16 Kelly McGonigal, *The Upside of Stress* (New York: Avery, 2016).

17 Steve Bradt, "Wandering Mind Not a Happy Mind," *The Harvard Gazette* (2010), https://news.harvard.edu/gazette/story/2010/11/wandering-mind-not-a-happy-mind/.

18 Harvard Medical School, Focus More to Ease Stress, https://www.health.harvard.edu/healthbeat/focus-more-to-ease-stress.

19 Kermit Pattison, "Worker, Interrupted: The Cost of Task Switching," *Fast Company* (July 28, 2008), https://www.fastcompany.com/944128/worker-interrupted-cost-task-switching.

20 Mayo Oshin, "9 Ways Multitasking Is Killing Your Brain and Productivity, According to Neuroscientists," *The Ladders* (September 10, 2018), https://www.theladders.com/career-advice/9-ways-multitasking-is-killing-your-brain-and-productivity-according-to-neuroscientists.

21 Stephanie Booth, "How Stress Can Shrink Your Brain and 6 Ways to Keep It from Happening," *Healthline* (November 21, 2018), https://www.healthline.com/health-news/how-stress-can-shrink-your-brain.

22 To Multitask or Not to Multitask, https://appliedpsychologydegree.usc.edu/blog/to-multitask-or-not-to-multitask/.

23 Shira Offer, Barbara Schneider, "Revisiting the Gender Gap in Time-Use Patterns: Multitasking and Well-Being among Mothers and Fathers in Dual-Earner Families," *American Sociological Review* 76, no. 6 (December 1, 2011), https://journals.sagepub.com/doi/abs/10.1177/0003122411425170.

24 John Brandon, You Touch This Gadget 2,617 Times Per Day. Here's How to Stop, Inc., https://www.inc.com/john-brandon/you-touch-this-gadget-2617-times-per-day-heres-how-to-stop.html.

25 Peter Frost et al., "An Examination of the Potential Lingering Effects of Smartphone Use on Cognition," *Applied Cognitive Psychology* 33, no. 6 (November/December 2019), https://onlinelibrary.wiley.com/doi/abs/10.1002/acp.3546.

26 Jesse Hicks, *What to Do When Your Phone Is Eroding Your Mental Health*, VICE.com, https://www.vice.com/en_us/article/d3a4bz/can-being-on-your-phone-cause-depression.

27 Angela Duckworth, *Grit: The Power of Passion and Perseverance* (New York: Scribner, 2016).

28 Limbic System, Realizations, Inc., https://arlenetaylor.org/brain-references/brain-and-nervous-system/human-brain/1678-limbic-system.

29 Travis Bradberry, Jean Greaves, with Patrick M. Lencioni, *Emotional Intelligence 2.0* (San Diego: TalentSmart, 2009).

30 About Emotional Intelligence, TalentSmart, https://www.talentsmart.com/about/emotional-intelligence.php.

31 Uncertainty Can Cause More Stress Than Inevitable Pain, *Science Daily* (March 29, 2016), https://www.sciencedaily.com/releases/2016/03/160329101037.htm.

32 Travis Bradberry, Jean Greaves, with Patrick M. Lencioni, *Emotional Intelligence 2.0* (San Diego: TalentSmart, 2009).

33 Nansook Park et al., "Positive Psychology and Physical Health: Research and Applications," *American Journal of Lifestyle Medicine* 10, no. 3 (May/June 2016): 200–06, https://www.ncbi.nlm.nih.gov/pmc/articles/PMC6124958/.

34 Charles S. Carver, Michael F. Scheier, and Suzanne C. Segerstrom, "Optimism," *Clinical Psychology Review* 30, no. 7 (November 2010): 879–89.

35 Scott Barry Kaufman, "Which Character Strengths Are Most Predictive of Well-Being?" *Beautiful Minds* (August 2, 2015), https://blogs.scientificamerican.com/beautiful-minds/which-character-strengths-are-most-predictive-of-well-being/.

36 Jim Silwa, "A Grateful Heart Is a Healthier Heart," American Psychological Association (April 9, 2015), https://www.apa.org/news/press/releases/2015/04/grateful-heart.

37 Gratitude Is Good Medicine, UC Davis Health Center (November 25, 2015), https://health.ucdavis.edu/medicalcenter/features/2015-2016/11/20151125_gratitude.html.

38 Rick Hanson, *Hardwiring Happiness* (New York: Harmony, 2013).

39 Research Claims Botox Makes People Happier, WalesOnline (April 1, 2019), https://www.walesonline.co.uk/news/wales-news/research-claims-botox-makes-people-2109187.

40 Stress Relief from Laughter? It's No Joke, Mayo Clinic, https://www.mayoclinic.org/healthy-lifestyle/stress-management/in-depth/stress-relief/art-20044456.

41 Steven Southwick and Dennis Charney, Resilience: *The Science of Mastering Life's Greatest Challenges* (United Kingdom: Cambridge University Press, 2018).

42 Nicole Spector, Smiling Can Trick Your Brain into Happiness—And Boost Your Health, Better, (November 28, 2017), https://www.nbcnews.com/better/health/smiling-can-trick-your-brain-happiness-boost-your-health-ncna822591.

43 Madhav Goyal et al., "Meditation Programs for Psychological Stress and Well-being," *JAMA Internal Medicine* 174, no. 3 (March 2014): 357–68, https://jamanetwork.com/journals/jamainternalmedicine/fullarticle/1809754.

44 Leo Widrich, 4 Practical Facts About the Human Brain That Can Help You Cultivate Emotional Resilience, *Fast Company* (March 29, 2019), https://www.fastcompany.com/90326620/emotional-resilience-and-the-brain.

45 What Is the Vagus Nerve in Meditation? Scottsdale Institute for Health and Medicine, https://www.stressbeaters.com/what-is-the-vagus-nerve-in-meditation/.

46 Sharon Salzburg (March 17, 2020), https://tricycle.org/wp-content/uploads/2020/04/Sharon-Salzberg_Zoom-practice-3_17_30.pdf.

47 Mindfulness STOP Skill (June 18, 2014), http://cogbtherapy.com/mindfulness-meditation-blog/mindfulness-stop-skill.

48 Rick Hanson with Forrest Hanson, *Resilient: How to Grow an Unshakable Core of Calm, Strength, and Happiness* (New York: Harmony Books, 2018).

49 Kristin D. Neff and Katie A. Dahm, Self-Compassion: What It Is, What It Does, And How It Relates to Mindfulness, https://self-compassion.org/wp-content/uploads/publications/Mindfulness_and_SC_chapter_in_press.pdf.

50 Jason Marsh, The Power of Self-Compassion, *Greater Good Magazine* (March 14, 2012), https://greatergood.berkeley.edu/article/item/the_power_of_self_compassion.

51 Kristin Neff and Christopher Germer, The Transformative Effects of Mindful Self-Compassion, Mindful (January 29, 2019), https://www.mindful.org/the-transformative-effects-of-mindful-self-compassion/.

52 Shannon Mehner, Kindness Is Contagious, New Study Finds, *Helix* (April 21, 2010), https://helix.northwestern.edu/article/kindness-contagious-new-study-finds.

53 Shawn Achor Shares the Single Greatest Predictor of Success, *Happiness and Longevity*, https://www.txconferenceforwomen.org/shawn-achor-shares-the-single-greatest-predictor-of-success-happiness-and-longevity/.

54 Loneliness Is as Harmful to Health as Smoking, Obesity, (August 28, 2019), https://www.ssmhealth.com/blogs/ssm-health-matters/august-2019/loneliness-social-isolation-harmful-to-health.

55 Ibid.

56 Gratitude Is Good Medicine, UC Davis Health Center (November 25, 2015), https://health.ucdavis.edu/medicalcenter/features/2015-2016/11/20151125_gratitude.html.

57 Katie Hanson, What Exactly Is Hope and How Can You Measure It?, http://positivepsychology.org.uk/hope-theory-snyder-adult-scale/.

58 Jill G. Hayhurst, John A. Hunter, and Ted Ruffman,"Encouraging Flourishing Following Tragedy: The Role of Civic Engagement in Well-Being and Resilience," *New Zealand Journal of Psychology* 47, no. 1 (April 2019), https://www.psychology.org.nz/wp-content/uploads/NZJP-Vol-48-No-1-DRAFT-v2-1.pdf#page=75.

59 Kelly McGonigal, *The Science of Compassion: A Modern Approach for Cultivating Empathy, Love, and Connection* (Sounds True: Unabridged edition (September 1, 2016).

60 The Health Benefits of Volunteering, Corporation for National and Community Service, https://www.nationalservice.gov/pdf/07_0506_hbr.pdf.

61 The Mirror Neuron Revolution: Explaining What Makes Humans Social, *Scientific American* (July 1, 2008), https://www.scientificamerican.com/article/the-mirror-neuron-revolut/.

62 Study: Exercise Has Long-Lasting Effect on Depression, https://today.duke.edu/2000/09/exercise922.html.

63 World Health Organization, Physical Activity and Adults, https://www.who.int/dietphysicalactivity/factsheet_adults/en/.

64 Amanda MacMillian,"You Need To Deal With Your Work Stress. Here's How," *Time* (February 9, 2019), https://time.com/4665623/exercise-work-stress-sleep/.

65 Ariana Huffington, *The Sleep Revolution: Transforming Your Life, One Night at a Time* (New York: Harmony Books, 2017).

66 Advanced Sleep Medicine Services, CDC Declares Sleep Disorders a Public Health Epidemic, https://www.sleepdr.com/the-sleep-blog/cdc-declares-sleep-disorders-a-public-health-epidemic/.

67 Ibid.

68 Alan Kohll, "New Study Shows Correlation between Employee Engagement and the Long-Lost Lunch Break," *Forbes* (May 29, 2018), https://www.forbes.com/sites/alankohll/2018/05/29/new-study-shows-correlation-between-employee-engagement-and-the-long-lost-lunch-break/#5349f15b4efc.

69 *Time Magazine: The Age of Anxiety*, special edition 2020, https://time.com/tag/anxiety/.

70 Six Seconds: The Emotional Intelligence Network, https://www.6seconds.org/2017/12/14/daniel-goleman-emotions-wellbeing-mindfulness/; and Richard J. Davidson, *Altered Traits: Science Reveals How Meditation Changes Your Mind, Brain, and Body* (New York: Avery, 2017).

71 Women's Long Work Hours Linked to Alarming Increases in Cancer, Heart Disease (June 16, 2016), https://www.sciencedaily.com/releases/2016/06/160616071935.htm.

72 Sheryl Sandberg and Adam Grant, *Option B: Facing Adversity, Building Resilience, and Finding Joy* (New York: Knopf, 2017).

73 Nina Zipkin, "Want to Sleep Better? Find Your Purpose," *Entrepreneur* (July 10, 2017), https://www.entrepreneur.com/article/297046.

74 Priyanka Aribindi, "J.K. Rowling's 10 Most Inspiring Quotes," *Time* (July 29, 2016), https://time.com/4421601/jk-rowling-inspirational-quotes/.

75 Zameena Maja, Actor Will Smith in Viral Video: "Failure Is a Massive Part of Being Able to Be Successful," MSNBC (January 24, 2018).

76 Gill Corkindale, "Overcoming Imposter Syndrome," *Harvard Business* Review (May 7, 2008), https://hbr.org/2008/05/overcoming-imposter-syndrome.

77 Lydia Craig, Are You Suffering from Imposter Syndrome? *International Journal of Behavioral Science* (September 2018), https://www.apa.org/science/about/psa/2018/09/imposter-syndrome.

78 Valerie Young, *The Secret Thoughts of Successful Women: Why Capable People Suffer from the Impostor Syndrome and How to Thrive in Spite of It* (New York: Crown Business, 2011).

79 Brené Brown, *Daring Greatly: How the Courage to Be Vulnerable Transforms the Way We Live, Love, Parent, and Lead* (New York: Avery, 2012).

80 Jenna Goudreau, "A Harvard Psychologist Says People Judge You Based on 2 Criteria When They First Meet You," *Business Insider* (January 16, 2016), https://www.businessinsider.com/harvard-psychologist-amy-cuddy-how-people-judge-you-2016-1.

81 Stephanie O. Lopez, "Vulnerability in Leadership: The Power of the Courage to Descend," *Industrial-Organizational Psychology Dissertations* 16 (January 1, 2018), https://pdfs.semanticscholar.org/6b04/c6a5cbdbf6d9bf00ec84a318cabeb18247ff.pdf.

82 Christian Jarrett, The "Beautiful Mess" Effect: Other People View Our Vulnerability More Positively Than We Do," *Research Digest* (August 2, 2018), https://digest.bps.org.uk/2018/08/02/the-beautiful-mess-effect-other-people-view-our-vulnerability-more-positively-than-we-do/.